By JOYCE EAGLESTONE

Bradford Libraries and
Information Service

© Joyce Eaglestone 1990
All rights reserved

British Library Cataloguing in Publication Data
Eaglestone, Joyce
The story tellers.
1. West Yorkshire (England). Social life. History, 1837
I. Title II. Bradford Libraries and Information Service
942.81708
ISBN 0-907734-24-3

Published by Bradford Libraries and Information Service
Central Library, Prince's Way, Bradford BD1 1NN, West Yorks.

Printed by Bradford Council Printing Unit

Front cover: Granny Downes and Lena

Preface and Dedication

My first title for this book was THE STORY TELLER: GRANNY.

As the work developed I began to realise that though it was mostly about her life, much of the information came from that other story teller, Mother.

The number of times she has said to me, "If only I could write."

Well, she did not need to write while she could talk, and she talked and remembered up to her ninety-seventh year.

As my Granny talked to me so my Mother talked to her grandchildren and great-grandchildren and it is for them that I have written this book. To get the facts right, for it is their history and their heritage.

So I dedicate this book to the story tellers, to those people who take time to talk of the past and so bring a richer pattern to all our lives.

Joyce Eaglestone

Contents

	Page
Preface and Dedication	iii
Illustrations	vi
Acknowledgement	vii

Chapter		Page
1	"He knew Patrick Brontë well, did my father."	1
2	"Send for Zillah!"	7
3	Enter 'Lena	11
4	The finest funeral Allerton had ever known	17
5	Hard times	21
6	"Your Dad ... saved my reason."	27
7	"In spite of everything it was a good year!"	31
8	"Don't call me 'Baby'!"	37
9	"I'll never go to Heaven; I've told so many lies!"	41
10	"She was always there."	47
11	Mollie	51
12	"I cry a bit and I pray."	57
13	"Been to never-leave-school, 'ave yer?"	61
14	Toller Lane	67
15	Granny sitters	71
16	"Those infernal machines!"	75
17	The topsy-turvy world of war	79
18	"Please, God, take me home."	85
19	The Family	89

Illustrations

The Story Tellers: Granny Downes and Lena	Cover
Rev. Patrick Brontë	Page 1
The Redmans, *chart*	4
Grandma Redman and Hannah Maria	7
Redman's Dining Rooms	9
Aunt Hagah	11
Granny's Family, *chart*	13
Albert House at the wheel	22
Claud and Percy Pickles	24
George and Madelena Hanson	31
House in West Park Road	34
Mollie and Joyce	40
Girlington Area, *map*	42
Dr Whitely as John Bull	51
Enoch and Emily Hanson	63
Fire Fighters	80
Joyce marries	83

(**Note.** All illustrations are the property of the author, except for that of Reverend Patrick Brontë and the map, which are provided courtesy of Bradford Libraries and Information Service.)

Acknowledgement

I would like to acknowledge the help given to me by Miss Elvira Willmott and Mr Robert Duckett of the Bradford Libraries and Information Service in the preparation of this book.

Joyce Eaglestone
Autumn 1990

Chapter 1 *"He knew Patrick Brontë well, did my father."*

Rev. Patrick Brontë

Long before I knew who the Brontës really were I had heard all about them from my Granny.

"My father saw them flitting from Thornton to Haworth with all their furniture on two flat carts," she told me. "He knew Patrick Brontë well, did my father."

Granny was a great story teller with a vivid turn of phrase.

"She were fine off and bonny donned," she would say of a smartly dressed woman.

"He's wirin' in," was her way of describing greed whether for food or for life.

Although Granny was sixty-seven when I was born she was often my companion and playmate. I well remember the day I acquired my blackboard and easel, I was the bossy teacher, Granny, the reluctant pupil.

At last she protested. "I'm fed up wi' doing summin'."

"Right," I said, "I'll show you how to do joined up writing."

"Nay, love, I reckon it's too late. I never had much schooling for they sent me to work in the spinning before I was seven." Granny had a way of looking beyond me with those slightly near set eyes, as if to a world I could never understand. "Mind, they sent me home again, said I was too little. After that I'd to take dinner in a basket to the two Josephs when they worked in Springholes Quarry near't Rock and Heifer pub."

I already knew about her two half brothers, Joe Redman and Joe Hainsworth, and the rest of the family who lived at 'top o't hill at Thornton.

Granny's father, William Redman, had moved there from his native Burnley in Lancashire. In his early years he was a hand loom weaver who kept his loom in his children's bedroom and carried his pieces (lengths of cloth) on his back to the Piece Hall in Bradford.

I never knew what year he moved, if he went alone or with his family, but he was certainly living in Thornton when Patrick Brontë was curate of the old Bell Chapel.

Patrick, his wife, Maria, and their two infant daughters had moved from Hartshead to Thornton on the 19th May 1815, just a month before the Battle of Waterloo.

John Schofield Firth, the then owner of Kipping Hall, seems to have had some influence in bringing Patrick Brontë to Thornton, and his daughter soon became friends with the curate's young wife.

Miss Firth kept a diary and it is her jottings, though brief, which shed some light on the neglected area of the Brontë years in Thornton.

An entry dated 9th June 1815 reads, 'We met Mr Brontë's family at Mr Kay's.'

This meeting would have taken place at Allerton Hall, now no longer in existence, for not long before this date Benjamin Kaye had bought the house and had settled there with his wife, Mercy.

Mr Kaye was a cotton manufacturer who gave out work to the cottagers in the area and who marketed his goods in Manchester. Mercy Kaye was the daughter of Mr Taylor of Stanbury and it is possible that through this link Patrick Brontë later moved to Haworth. Certainly it was a Mr Taylor who sent the two flat carts, with drivers, to move the Brontë possessions to Haworth.

During the five years that they lived in Thornton the four youngest Brontë children were born in the Glebe house in Market Street. This was the site of the ancient township mentioned in the Domesday Book.

At that time the new Turnpike road through Thornton had not been built and this old highway would take all the traffic.

Mrs Brontë's drawing room was at the back of this house and this was used as her lying-in room, away from the noise of market carts. From this house my great grandfather saw the Brontë children taken out for an airing.

Soon after the youngest child, Anne, was born, Maria Brontë made that long trip which was probably her last, for she died the next year.

Later Patrick Brontë came back to Thornton to read the burial service for his old friend, John Schofield Firth. Some years later Charlotte Brontë stayed at Allerton Hall where Mercy Kaye nursed her back to health after her terrible experience at Cowan Bridge School when her two eldest sisters died.

It is said she occasionally visited the Kayes and so was seen in Thornton.

William Redman was to take an almost paternal interest in the Brontë family for the rest of their lives and was very proud of this tenuous link with them.

William had lived through terrible times when his first wife, Hagah, became ill with cholera. She died leaving him with four children, Ann, Elizabeth, Ben and Joseph.

In those days the families of such victims were treated as outcasts and he never forgot this sense of rejection. Later if he heard of a family similarly afflicted he would do all he could to help, taking food, even helping to nurse the dying.

Afterwards he would go straight to his cellar and wash and change into clean clothing before going back to his own family.

Later he married Maria Hainsworth, an unmarried woman who already had two sons, Joseph and Charles, so that between them they had six children, two who were named Joseph. The two boys were called big Joe and little Joe.

Maria had two daughters by William, Hagah, named for William's first wife, much to the chagrin of Maria, and Zillah, my granny. She was born on the 9th April 1853 in the end house, Long Row, Hill Top, Thornton. They termed their combined family, thine, mine and ours.

Two years after Granny was born Charlotte Brontë died.

By then life in Thornton had changed dramatically. Hand loom weavers had been thrown out of work but quarries and mines were working full time to supply building materials for houses and factories, and fuel for steam engines.

William had always been a follower of Wesley but now the nonconformists were established and had become respectable, and as he played the double bass he travelled widely to play at anniversaries.

He had always kept in touch with his relatives in Burnley, the Bannisters, and he would go back there to play at the chapel. Granny told me of the many times as a little girl she had walked with him across the moor to Burnley helping him carry his unwieldly instrument.

The Redmans were a musical family. Ben Redman played the cello and they also owned a piano. William now worked for Dr Rawson as an agent and collector. In those days people would pay a penny or twopence a week to the doctor so that they would be cared for in times of illness. He would also collect money owed to the doctor.

He must have had some education to do this work and it has always seemed strange to me that he was so casual about his little daughter's education. For

THE REDMANS

William REDMAN

1st wife **Hagah**		*2nd wife* **Maria Hainsworth**
children	*Maria's children before marriage*	*children*

1st wife's children:

1. **Ben**
   a quarryman
   17 children
   (11 survived)

2. **Joseph**
   ('Big Joe')
   Killed in quarry accident.
   Married Ann

3. **Elizabeth**
   married INGHAM
   - children

4. **Ann**
   married ROBINSON
   - children

Maria's children before marriage:

1. **Joseph Hainsworth**
   ('Little Joe')
   builder
   Married 'Big Joe's' widow, Ann Redman
   - 11 children including Hannah Maria

2. **Charlie Hainsworth**

2nd wife's children:

1. **Hagah**

2. **Zillah** ('Granny')
   see separate chart on page 13.

4

though Granny could just about sign her name she could do little more than spell out the headlines in the newspaper.

Perhaps he thought that girls did not need education, but I find it hard to understand how he could allow a child under seven to be sent to work.

I do not know at what age Granny started to work in the mill but no doubt her first job was as a spinner and then later she became a weaver.

According to her marriage certificate she married Joseph Downes on 24th November 1875 at Bradford Registry Office. She was twenty-two and her bridegroom who was a year younger was a delver and the son of a farmer. William Redman's occupation was entered as Agent.

The two witnesses who put crosses in place of a signature were John and Harriet Ann Drake. If the Bible dates are to be believed the marriage took place only just in time, for Fred Downes was born on the 7th December 1875.

The second child, Alice, was born within the next two years.

It seemed that Joseph Downes came from a family already tainted with the dread disease, tuberculosis. His work in the quarry would not have helped and unlike miners, who work the year round, quarry work was seasonal. In a bad winter workers would be laid off for months.

Granny did not talk much of those early years of her marriage but I know she lived at Hill Top in Thomson Fold. This over-looked the valley and from there she watched men working on the railway viaduct which took the train to Queensbury.

She could see Thornton station being built and was there at the opening of the railway on the 14th October 1878.

By then little Freddie would have died and not long afterwards Joseph Downes succumbed to the dreaded disease; so that Granny was a widow before she was twenty-five.

Before another year had passed her father William Redman had died.

He had been a member of a friendly society called *The Ancient Order of Foresters.* At the death of a member all those who lived in the area would follow the coffin carrying a small branch from a tree.

The procession filled the narrow road from the house at Hill Top to the non-conformist graveyard and as each member filed past the open grave he dropped his branch onto the coffin so that the grave was filled to the top with branches.

Granny would weep when she told me of that day for she had been devoted to her father.

Chapter 2 "Send for Zillah!"

Grandma Redman and Hannah Maria

In these years Granny's half brothers and sisters had moved away from Thornton with the exception of her mother's son, Charlie Hainsworth. All I know of him is that he had become something of a wastrel and a drunkard, 'a nowt', according to Granny.

Many years before Joseph Redman had been killed in the quarry and his stepbrother 'little' Joe Hainsworth had married the widow, Ann. He had left the quarry to become a builder and much of the cottage property he built at Mountain, near Queensbury, and in Allerton is still standing.

He now lived in Allerton with his wife and the survivors of their eleven children, the eldest, Billie, and the youngest Hannah Maria.

William Redman's two daughters by his first marriage, Ann and Elizabeth, had married, Ann to a man called Robinson, and she lived in the Queensbury area. Elizabeth was now Mrs Ingham and I believe she lived in Allerton.

Ben Redman had moved to Heaton and was overseer quarryman at Heaton Royds Quarry behind Toller Lane. He lived at North Hall Farm near Heaton Woods and ran a small holding, but he was continually short of money, especially when the quarter's rent had to be paid.

His wife bore him seventeen children but only eleven survived, and the older children used to cheer when a baby died. Ben sent his daughters to a private school in Heaton.

I am not quite sure why Maria Redman and her two daughters decided to move to Allerton. Perhaps her son, Charlie Hainsworth, had become a problem or maybe she was offered a cottage by her other son, Joseph, who owned much property in the area.

Mother said that one of the reasons was that work was more plentiful in Allerton. Granny and Aunt Hagah soon found work in their new home while their mother looked after Granny's surviving child, Alice Downes.

Granny always called her Alice Downes and she was a part of my childhood, as real to me as any member of my family. According to Granny she was an angel, good and patient and perfect in every way, but frail like her father and brother.

Mother said that when they moved to Allerton there was no Anglican church and people met in private houses. By then Granny had become an Anglican though her sister, Hagah, remained faithful to Methodism to the end of her life.

Perhaps those first years in Allerton were pleasant ones for Maria Redman with her two daughters and little Alice. I have a charming photograph of her taken with Joseph Hainsworth's daughter, Hannah Maria, another grandchild.

Then Alice Downes became ill. She was coming up to ten at the time and at first it seemed no more than a cold as winter came on. Granny was convinced it was caused by sitting on wet grass at the November bonfire, but the family Bible shows she did not die until March the following year.

I used to weep when Granny told me about Alice Downes, that perfect child. Within a year of her death there were more tears to shed, for their mother, Maria Redman, died.

The sisters had worn mourning for nine long years and it must have seemed a chill and lonely world to them. They were so very different. At thirty-three Granny was small and slim and pleasure loving. Hagah was three years older and very serious.

At that time they heard of two sisters called Jowett who had opened a dining room in Bradford. A trip to Bradford in those days must have been something of an adventure for with the coming of the Industrial Revolution it had become known as the Chicago of the north.

Perhaps the sisters were weary of weaving and of working for the long hours, perhaps they needed a change. After much discussion they decided to use their small savings to open a dining room.

They rented a shop, 58 Thornton Road in Bradford and called it Redman's Dining Rooms, and they furnished the front part with long tables and benches.

Here they served between sixty and a hundred dinners each day to workmen and to some of the business gentlemen of the town. A roast beef dinner cost a shilling, (five pence) and half that price would buy a portion of meat and potato pie with peas. Jam roly-poly or rice pudding cost three pence.

Redman's Dining Rooms today (now Walker's)

When they first opened the shop all the cooking was done in a coal oven and on the open fire, but later they bought a gas cooker. Sixty pounds of beef was bought each week. Once when Granny was standing on a stool trying to unhook it from the ceiling she fell with the whole lot on her arm.

She never thought to see a doctor and though she didn't realise it she had broken her arm and it set crooked and was painful for the rest of her life.

There were sacks of potatoes to be peeled each evening, peas to be put to soak and pastry to mix. Each day the wooden tables were scrubbed and also the flagged floor which had to be sanded in bad weather.

As well as dinners they served mugs of tea at breakfast time for men who would bring their own sandwiches. They also took lodgers and sometimes had four men sleeping in the attic. It was hard work from morning to night and even on Sunday the lodgers had to be fed.

At first the sisters worked alone but later they employed young maids who came from the country or the mining areas where there was no work for girls. For 3s. 6d. (less than twenty pence) and their keep they would work all hours. They arrived untrained and under fed but that was soon remedied for there was no shortage of good food at the dining rooms.

Some girls moved on to better jobs but one girl stayed for many years and only left to be married.

The first mill had been built in the town in 1800 and in spite of machine breaking and troubles when the Riot Act had to be read, trade had increased by the end of the century.

Workers had come from all parts of the British Isles and particularly from Ireland. To house these workers millowners had dwelling houses built adjacent to the factories. Sanitation was not considered important and sometimes many families had to share one privy, or earth closet.

Some mill owners paid in special coin which had to be spent at the mill shops where food was often adulterated, sand added to sugar, flour running with weevils.

In the early days the mill owners would also live close to the factories but later when pollution increased they moved further out of town to large houses in great contrast to the squalid workers' dwellings.

Fortunes were made, and lost, and made again. 'Rags to rags in three generations' was a common saying.

Sometimes large and extended families would move into one area, and one Irish family lived near the dining rooms. They were a problem family and though the police were loathe to get involved with the wife beatings and fighting my granny had no such inhibitions.

She would go in there to bring babies and to lay out the dead and to act as a rough and ready family guidance service when the wakes got out of hand.

She was well under five foot in height and slim, but when the cry went up, "Send for Zillah," she would go in there, quite unafraid.

There were areas of Bradford where the police would only patrol in pairs but Granny went wherever she was needed, quite unafraid and safe.

By now she had reverted to her maiden name of Redman. The Miss Redmans were known and liked. The dining rooms were doing so well that the men had to be there early to get a place at the long tables.

In spite of the punishing work I reckon they were happy for neither sister was afraid of hard work. Aunt Hagah went to the Methodist church, Granny to the Parish church which later became the cathedral.

Bradford was an exciting place to live with its theatres, its markets and the sisters were making money and, better still, they were saving it.

Chapter 3 Enter 'Lena

Aunt Hagah

The old *Bradford Illustrated* shows that Bradford in 1889 was a thriving place. Food was getting more interesting. Yorkshire Relish could be bought in bottles costing 6d (2½p). Goodhalls had invented custard powder and jelly squares. Tordoff's tea was on sale, 'the best and cheapest and blended by special machinery using steam power.'

The 'St John' camera could be bought at Messrs Percy Lund & Co for £3.10s. A firm called Hemingway had invented New Electric Fire Lighters said to be magical and cheaper than wood.

There were photographic studios, and possibly before having the likeness taken it would have been wise to purchase Jowett's hair stainer. This would 'improve with washing which is an advantage to its use on whiskers.'

The Globe Parcel Express would send packages to any part of the country and to the continent, to India, China, Japan and America.

There was a school of shorthand in Sunbridge Road with a separate room for ladies! For just £21 the Hammond Typewriter could be bought with one extra type-wheel, and in a mahogany or black walnut case.

The Bradford Union Advance Bank would lend money, £20 to £10,000, with easy repayments and strictest privacy guaranteed.

Surgeon dentists advertised painless extractions and Messrs Forshaw and Ellison of Westgate would supply artificial teeth at 3s 6d, 5s and 7s 6d per tooth, and even resorted to poetry!

> We've found the teeth that people get
> When time destroys the natural set
> No longer need you mumble here
> Or bolt your food in pain and fear.
> These teeth are strong, and not alone
> They'll rend the flesh and pick the bone
> But masticate the food aright
> And indigestion put to flight.

It enlarges on this theme at some length.

So they came to this place, those seeking work or wealth or excitement or even those hoping to start a new life in a different place as the two Redman sisters had done.

One such stranger was a teenager from Scotland, young Will Ross, and he rented the front attic above Redman's Dining Rooms. Very soon he became a favourite with them all. He was an engineer and he started to work with one Albert House who had a small works in Hustlergate. Later they became partners.

Albert House was the son of a journeyman boilermaker who was now making cycles in a yard off Hustlgate. He lived in Lee Street near the dining rooms with his wife and young family.

" 'ouse were allus a clever 'ead," Granny used to say. She always called him 'ouse. He really was a very clever mechanic and with this skill should have gone far in the motor trade.

Unfortunately money seemed to slip through his fingers and many a time Granny or Aunt Hagah would carry a basket of food round to Lee Street when there was no housekeeping money for his wife.

Twice Granny saved him from bankruptcy, money which was never repaid. After this Will Ross broke up the partnership and started his own garage at Ben Rhydding. The firm Ross Bros is still there. He married an orphan like himself and took on a ready made family, his wife's brothers and sister.

I know very little of Granny's life in those early years. The two sisters must have had a somewhat stormy relationship for they were completely different. I do know that Granny had a man friend who worked as a joiner.

When disaster struck and Granny became pregnant, he did not offer to marry her.

GRANNY'S FAMILY

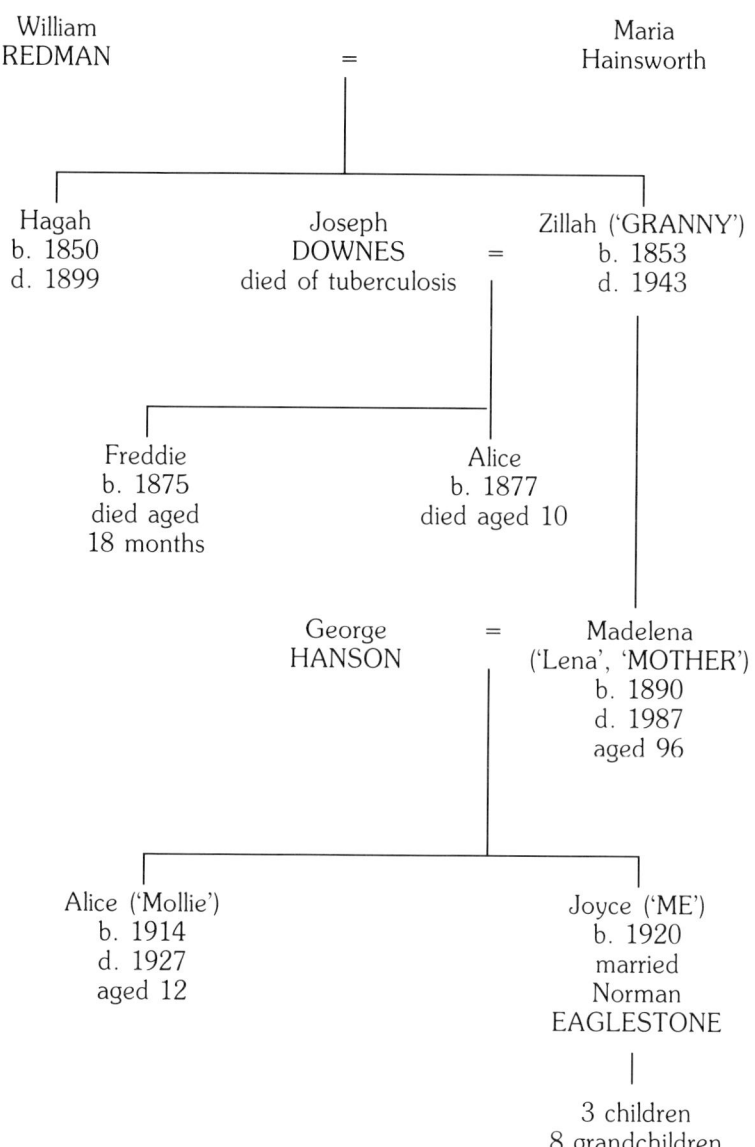

Note: See chart on page 4 for REDMAN and HAINSWORTH families.

This was one area of her life Granny never mentioned at all and all I know came from my mother who was born on the 17th July 1890 at Beggerington Square, Northowram, which was the home of Granny's half sister, Ann Robinson.

The baby's birth was registered in Halifax some weeks later. It seemed Granny had visited the theatre in her late months of pregnancy and the heroine had been called Madelena, and so that became her baby's name.

Mother told me that when she was ten days old Granny brought her to Thornton, walking all the way. I don't know if that was really true or just poetic licence, for it would have been possible to catch a train.

Granny put her baby to nurse with Mrs Drake of Hill Top Farm who was possibly the same Mrs Drake who had witnessed her marriage to Joe Downes some fifteen years before.

From there Granny made her way back to the dining rooms. It must have been a sad and lonely time for her for she would have had no sympathy from Aunt Hagah.

Mrs Drake had older children who used to take the baby out to play in the barn and one day they let her fall from a higher area onto the flagged floor. They picked her up unconscious and for the rest of her life she had a flat area at the back of her head.

"I was always a dunce at school," Mother told me, "and I reckon it was because of that fall."

When Mother was about eighteen months old Mammy Drake, as she called her foster mother, developed breast cancer and was too ill to care for her. Mother actually seemed to remember leaving the farm, how the old lady had wrapped her up warmly and sent her to Bradford on the milk cart.

Tears always came to her eyes when she spoke of her life at the farm and her dear Mammy Drake for it was the only home she knew.

Life at the dining rooms was very different. There was no time to care for a toddler and she was definitely unwanted, especially by Aunt Hagah who seemed to blame her for the situation.

"You're a nowt and never should have been born," she was told regularly. She was compared constantly with the angelic Alice Downes and beloved little Freddie.

Mother remembers being lifted onto a stool by the old stone sink and set to wash up. She had to eat her dinner with the men who constantly teased her. One day a man peppered her plate of dinner and she threw the whole lot at him.

She was soundly thrashed for that by Aunt Hagah. There were more slaps than kisses and for the rest of her life she was desperately searching for love and never quite finding it.

Before she was three Mother was sent to Carlton Street school which seemed a long walk for her. At first she went with the House children for Cissie House was just about the same age and they remained friends until Cissie's death. Later when the House family moved away she had to go to school alone.

There seems to have been a religious power struggle between the two sisters with little Lena in between, for before long she had dropped the first part of her name. "They used to call me mad Lena," she said. "I suppose I was a bit mad in those days for my hair was red."

It seems strange that Aunt Hagah wanted to take her unwanted niece to the Methodist church while Granny expected her to go to the parish church.

Apart from this Mother remembers Sunday as a good day when they had tea in the sitting room above the shop. That day they always used Aunt Hagah's tea service and I have it still, red, gold and turquoise china, and far too fragile to use.

The little jug is stained brown for Aunt Hagah, that good Methodist, enjoyed rum in her tea on Sunday, though the tell-tale bottle was hidden away.

On Sunday afternoons my mother was allowed to look at the pictures in the family bible which is an enormous leather bound volume bought, I believe, at the time of Granny's marriage to Joseph Downes. That, and Bunyan's Select Works were the only books they possessed.

Mother came to enjoy living in the town. She would go with Granny and Aunt Hagah to the meat market which would be bright with flares until late on Saturday night when they would sell off the meat very cheaply.

She loved the spice market and the shop in Westgate where Judy Barrett sold her humbugs. A lot was happening in Thornton Road, too.

In those days there were steps from the pavement leading down to the cellar and she would sit on the steps and watch the traffic. There was a brewery opposite and drays would be going in and out dragged by great carthorses.

Wagons rumbled past continually bringing coal from the mines and stone from the quarries. There were farmers driving carts carrying churns of milk, for this was delivered twice a day and ladled out into the customer's own jug.

Salt Jim came round with huge blocks of salt which had to be hammered into smaller pieces and then ground down to store in stone jars. She talked of another character she called Whistling Ben.

The best excitement of all was on days when there was a house fire for the fire station was quite near the dining rooms and Mother remembers the fire engines, pulled by galloping horses, skimming over cobbles made smooth by mud and horse dirt.

"Oh, how I used to love a fire, and the great bell ringing." She would smile when she talked of it, remembering. "I really did love the town."

To the end of her life Mother was a town sparrow.

Chapter 4 "It was the finest funeral Allerton had ever known."

By 1894 Albert House was well established as a cycle maker.

In the 1850's a certain Mrs Bloomer of New York had invented a costume for ladies. Later on divided skirts were proposed by the Rational Dress Society in the eighteen eighties.

Although such costumes had not become the rage in Bradford Albert House had a novel idea for bringing publicity and boosting cycle sales, so he built a bicycle for his wife, Elizabeth.

He decided that she would be the first woman in Bradford to ride a bicycle wearing bloomers and though Mrs House wept and pleaded to be spared this ordeal, such was his personality that she had to do as he wished.

It seemed that her fears were justified for when she appeared in her bloomers in the streets of Bradford she became a target for abuse and only just escaped actual mobbing.

Soon after this a Mr James Tuke brought the first motor car to Bradford. News of its coming brought such a wave of excitement that when it arrived in Market Street crowds of people were already waiting.

Mother remembered it though she was only six at the time.

Naturally Albert House was among the crowd and when Mr Tuke went to 'stable' his car in the New Inn yard Albert followed and offered a free place at his works. He suggested he might do any needed repairs.

Mr Tuke agreed and as he was already late for an appointment asked Albert to drive the car there. As Albert had no idea how to drive he got two men to push it while he steered.

According to his records this caused much excitement and amusement especially to the cab drivers along the way who, to quote, 'gave a running commentary in quaint, witty and strong language.'

The car was an Arnold Benz of approximately two and a half horse power. It only held three pints of petrol and its highest speed on a good road was twelve miles an hour, though to drive at such a pace was to break the law.

No horn was needed for when the car was running it could be heard a hundred yards away. Albert spent the next few days overhauling the engine and discovering just how everything worked and soon he was driving the car, though it was no easy ride.

There was so much vibration that many a passenger on a trip out decided to go back by train, or to walk.

Though he was interested in cars Albert continued to make bicycles and when his third child, also called Albert, was three years old he built him a small cycle so that he could ride beside his mother at the Stanley Cycle Show, and so he became the youngest cyclist in the world.

Before Albert's seventh child, Clarence, was walking, he had built an even smaller cycle with wheels just ten inches in diameter and the seat pillar seven and a half inches high. At the age of seventeen months Clarence was put on this bike and taught to ride.

At Christmas 1898 a pantomime was staged at the Bradford Theatre Royal. It was Jack the Giant Killer and Albert contrived more publicity for himself when he invited the actor who played the giant, Mr Picton Robinson, to wear Clarence's small bicycle on his watch chain.

Later at another cycle show at Belle Vue Barracks little Clarence again rode his bike. Mr Ernest Flowers, M.P., who opened the exhibition declared, "Of all forms of athletic recreation there is perhaps not one more valuable than cycling. Travelling improves the mind and enlarges the mental horizon and also improves muscles and stamina by exercise."

That same year Mr Flowers presented Clarence, as the youngest cyclist in the world, with an illuminated address and a gold medal. I doubt if Clarence appreciated the gift even though it was signed by Arthur Balfour, then Leader of the House of Commons, and many more important men.

Clarence's muscle and stamina were not improved by the exercise for he grew up very rickety and died at the age of twelve.

There was a great deal of excitement in Bradford and Mother was at the edge of it, but the good times were not to last.

Aunt Hagah became seriously ill and could no longer work. She had breast cancer and there was nothing they could do but sell out and go back to live in Allerton.

Hagah was not a patient invalid, and ill though she was, she stipulated that Mother must go the Wesleyan Sunday School. Mother refused. There was a great deal of unpleasantness and argument but Mother would not give way.

"If I can't go to St Peter's Sunday School I won't go at all," she said.

She never talked much about the next months except to say it was dreadful. Granny never spoke of it at all. She just nursed her sister day and night until the 5th June 1899 when Hagah died.

By then Granny was under five stone in weight but she used her remaining strength and dwindling savings to organise a really good funeral.

As she was not well enough to take Mother to buy her mourning in Bradford a neighbour went with her. Mother was a month off nine years old and insisted on having a hat with an ostrich feather.

Granny had hysterics when she saw the hat and heard how much it had cost, ten shillings and sixpence.

All Granny's family came to the funeral so there had to be many carriages to follow the hearse. Each vehicle was drawn by jet black horses and on all their heads were the impressive black plumes of mourning. Frail though Granny was she went out to inspect the horses to make sure that there was no trace of white on them.

Her dress was of such heavy silk that it would stand alone.

It would have been an impressive funeral anyway but the most exciting part of it for all the onlookers was when a motor car appeared at the street end and drew up behind the carriages.

Albert House and Will Ross 'dismounted'. Both were dressed in black frock coats and trousers with 'tall shiners' on their heads. The only touch of white was in their starched shirts and white wing collars.

It was the finest funeral Allerton had ever known, and not just Allerton, for Aunt Hagah was to be buried in Thornton with her parents. The procession made its way down Allerton Road to Four Lane Ends and so up to Thornton.

Mother said she was really someone in Allerton for long afterwards, but the months of nursing and final effort of organising the funeral caused Granny's complete collapse.

When she recovered a little she was taken to Burnley to be nursed by her father's relatives, the Bannisters. Perhaps they couldn't or wouldn't take a not quite nine-year-old child. Maybe Granny was too ill to care, but Mother was left in Allerton.

Once I asked her, "How on earth did you manage alone?"

"A little girl came in to sleep with me and the neighbours fed me," was her answer.

I do not know how many relatives lived in Allerton then, but I am sure that Hannah Maria Hainsworth would be there. Her mother, Ann, who had been Joe Redman's young widow, and had later borne eleven children to Joe Hainsworth, was a semi invalid who seemed to spend all her days in the wall bed in the kitchen.

Her daughter Hannah Maria had never gone out to work and even after her mother died she seemed to have enough money to live in one of the cottages her father had built.

Yet even in such a close community it seemed to me to be a dreadful thing for Granny to have left her child alone. Later when she recovered and came home my mother was left alone quite often, sometimes for weeks while Granny went off nursing the sick.

The year Aunt Hagah died the Boer War broke out on the 10th October. I doubt if Mother knew anything of that but she did remember the bonfire they had in Allerton on 28th February 1900 when Mafeking was relieved.

She also remembered the day Queen Victoria died a year later. They were now Edwardians.

Mother loved Sunday School but she hated school. "I was an awful dunce," she said, "I never could spell."

If you could not spell in those days you were branded as lazy and earned the cane. It was easy to earn the cane. One boy had it every morning for coming to school with dirty hands even though it was not his fault. His widowed mother couldn't afford to buy soap.

Like her mother before her Lena was left-handed but had been forced to write with her right hand. I think she might have been dyslexic, she was certainly word blind all her life.

For the three years after Hagah died somehow they coped. Granny had no source of income but she was one of those women who were useful in a village. She could bring babies and nurse and lay out the dead, would cook meals for people and mind children.

There was no doubt about it, she was hanging on for the great day when her unwanted child would be some use in the world and would begin to earn money instead of wasting her time at school.

It was not long before Lena became a 'half timer.'

Chapter 5 Hard Times

The 'half time' scheme was excellent for the mill owners who had an unlimited supply of cheap labour, and it was a help to parents who were desperately short of money and grateful that the children could contribute a few shillings to the family budget.

One week a child would start work at six o'clock and work until noon with a half hour break for breakfast. The afternoon would be spent in school. The next week they had morning school and the afternoon at work.

Mother desperately wanted to be apprenticed to a milliner but Granny said she had no money to pay the premium and no means to keep her, so at thirteen she had to work at the mill full time.

She did not so much mind working at spinning but later when she had to go into the weaving shed, for this paid better, she was very miserable for she hated the work.

There was little else a girl could do in a village like Allerton but work in the mill or go into service, and no self-respecting girl would do that.

Mother was a member of the Girls' Friendly Society and it was their policy to get the village girls to welcome the strangers who had come into the area to work as maids.

Through this scheme she became friendly with a girl called Lena Cole who worked in one of the big houses at Chellow Dene. She was allowed to have a girl visitor at weekends when other staff were out and my mother spent many evenings there.

They would eat what was left of the evening meal and then together wash the dishes. It was there Mother learned to love exotic and unusual food and to appreciate the pretty china and cut glass which she handled so carefully.

She had many friends in the village, girls she worked with, Lena Pickard who later went away to be a nurse, Lizzie Sweeting, Alice Howarth, whose family was a cut above the rest. Her best friend was Sophie Beasley, an orphan who came originally from London but had been sent to live with relations in Whitby.

Money had been left to keep her but the uncle who took Sophie to Whitby from London, and the uncle in Whitby, decided to celebrate this windfall. Together they drank away poor Sophie's legacy.

She was brought up in abject poverty and as there was no work for girls in Whitby the whole family moved to Allerton where she worked in the mill.

Unfortunately Sophie had a speech defect and could not pronounce the letter 's' so that to have her say her name was a nightmare. My mother took Sophie under her wing, pronounced her name for her and fended off the cruel ones who mocked.

They remained friends for life and Auntie Sophie was a lovely person.

Granny's extended family still lived in the area. There were the Inghams in Allerton, descendants of her half sister, Elizabeth, and more relations in Wilsden from the other sister, Ann Robinson.

They visited the Redmans at North Hall Farm and Mother sometimes stayed there for she was about the same age as Agnes, Ben's youngest child.

"We used to walk home at midnight sometimes when we'd been visiting them in Heaton," Mother told me.

Albert House and his family were still their friends. He had started the first public service motor coach and when he applied for a licence it was issued on a Steam Tram Car Driver's Licence with Steam crossed out and Motor written in.

When firms had staff outings they would hire his car, and it was the first car to be used in the parliamentary election in the Bradford, Shipley, Keighley and Skipton areas.

Albert House at the wheel

Later he was to bring the first aeroplane to Bradford on a flat cart, pulled by a horse, soon after Bleriot made his first channel crossing.

He was in Paris on business when Santos Dumont, a famous air pioneer made his first 'heavier than air' flight. In those days Albert was not at home much and once when his little daughter saw him come into the house she asked, "Who is that man?"

Dr Whitely figured largely in talk of the old days. Granny's sayings often began with, "Dr Whitely always said .... "

His coming to Allerton was due to Hannah Maria Hainsworth whose mother was related to his mother. When she heard he had just qualified she sent word to say that they needed a doctor in Allerton.

He had never wanted to be a doctor for his mother came from farming stock and he would have liked to be a farmer, but family pressure made him study medicine. He always looked more like a farmer to me.

He came as a bachelor and stayed so until he retired at the age of fifty-six, but he had a housekeeper, Mrs Lightfoot, a widow with a young daughter.

I believe it was soon after he arrived in Allerton that Granny became ill with dizzy spells when she would pass out for a while and would then be sick for days on end.

The doctor said it was dangerous for her to be alone in the house, and as Mother's wage was their only income she could not stay with her. I believe it was the doctor's idea that they should move to a larger house and share it with Hannah Maria, Mother's cousin, who was also in poor health.

She suffered from bouts of chest trouble and was convinced she had tuberculosis and would gasp for breath, but as she lived into her eighties I imagine she was an asthmatic.

It might have seemed a good idea but it turned out that, rather than caring for Granny, Hannah Maria expected Mother to care for her. Mother would rush home from the mill in her half hour for breakfast and take Granny her breakfast in bed. Hannah Maria expected to have her breakfast in bed, too, and was very unpleasant if she didn't get it.

In those days on Saturday mornings there was no weaving but the time was spent cleaning the looms. On Saturday afternoon Mother had to clean the house and do the washing.

Hannah Maria paid Mother a shilling a week for doing her washing.

To make matters more difficult Granny and Hannah Maria could not agree and quarrelled incessantly, two ill women, frustrated and believing they had not long to live.

In spite of all this Mother seems to have enjoyed life in the village for she was a member of the dramatic society at church and I have a picture of her as part of the chorus of an operetta. I imagine they would ask her just to mime the words for she was completely tone deaf. It was not that she just could not sing in tune but she had no idea how awful she sounded when she tried to sing.

While she was in her teens she became friendly with two handsome young men, Claude and Percy Pickles from Liverpool. They were either friends or relations of Hannah Maria and had called to see her when they came to Bradford as part of an orchestra, for they were both professional musicians.

Claude became Mother's particular friend and I have a card written by him on his return home, thanking them for their hospitality. They corresponded regularly for some years which must have been hard for Mother who hated letter writing. I do not know why the friendship ended.

Perhaps they lived too far from each other, or maybe it was because Granny hung round her daughter's neck like the proverbial albatross, or maybe it was just that Mother sang to Claude!

Claude and Percy Pickles

Her friendship with him put her off the local boys. She hated weaving and she hated the company she had to keep.

"You've no idea what it was like," she told me, 'the dreadful language, the vulgar way the men talked and tried to take liberties. We had to learn to kick out, and it was always the Labour men who were the worst."

To the end of her life she believed that the Labour party, bad language and bad behaviour were inextricably mixed.

Granny's health did not improve, and Mother had come to believe that it was only a matter of time before the end.

She had become friendly with a girl called Marjorie Kershaw who was a Mormon and Mother often went to church services with her. Marjorie was planning to emigrate to Salt Lake City, Utah, and though Mother had no intention of becoming a Mormon she decided that she would go with Marjorie when her mother died.

But Marjorie had to go alone. Granny did not die.

Chapter 6 "Your dad coming into my life just about saved my reason."

As far as I know there was no 'squire' in the Allerton area, but the Industrial Revolution had brought to the top very powerful and self made men, the mill owners.

Sir James Hill had started life in abject poverty and when he first married had lived in a small cottage in Clayton. With hard work and good fortune he had clawed his way up the ladder of industry, and in spite of becoming bankrupt at one stage, had ended up a very wealthy man.

He had sent his sons to boarding school and had married his daughter to one of the Amblers, another wealthy family.

Lady Hill, who had a park named for her in Allerton, never changed her way of speaking. One time when a friend was having some difficulty getting into her carriage Lady Hill was heard to give this piece of advice.

"Why don't you do as I do and get in arse first?"

Her grandson Geoffrey Ambler had his own private plane and would circle low over the houses. One of the family once said to me, "How I envied people who lived in an ordinary house in a road. I hated living in a big house with a high wall round the garden, it was so lonely."

Sir James Hill was Mayor of Bradford and so was another wealthy and self made man, David Wade. When King George V and Queen Mary visited Bradford the Wades were at the top table. Ice cream was offered as dessert and the King refused it.

Mrs David Wade leaned across and whispered, "Nay, Sir, it's a poor belly what wean't warm an ice!"

The mill owners must have seemed not so far removed from the King himself to some of his workers. Mother told me of one occasion when she was alone in the house and could not fasten the hooks at the back of her dress.

She put on a shawl and ran round to their next door neighbour and there in the kitchen was Ellen, who was soon to marry young Albert Hill. "I'll do up your hooks, Lena," she said cheerfully.

Mother told me in hushed tones. "And she became Ellen, Lady Hill."

Even in her old age if Mother happened to meet anyone remotely connected with the Hills or the Amblers she seemed to get a distinct weakness in her right knee, as if she felt a curtsey coming on.

Not long before she died Mother was grumbling about the expenses now paid to the Lord Mayors, particularly to the women who had to have a dress allowance. "In my day the Lord Mayor paid his own expenses," she said.

I protested, "But if they were poor men or women they couldn't become Lord Mayor unless they had financial help."

"If they are poor they've no right to be Lord Mayor," she said.

Life in Allerton must have been rather lonely for a man like the doctor. He was on call day and night and if he went to the theatre he always had to say where he would be and was often called out.

He was very often at their house to see Granny or Hannah Maria and Mother seemed to have rather a strange relationship with him. When she was telling me some anecdote of the past she would often say, "Oh, I'd fallen out with Dr Whitely at that time."

Only on one occasion did she tell me why she had quarrelled with him and that was when she was in his consulting room and had complained of toothache.

"I'll take it out for you," he said, getting a pair of forceps out of his desk drawer.

"Oh, no you won't."

"Oh, yes I will." There was an undignified chase round the room and then he stood with his back to the door barring her way.

I don't know how she escaped and she held this incident against him for a very long time. As the tooth continued to ache she asked a friend to send word to a dentist. In those days dentists would often travel round the district seeing patients in their own homes.

One day a young man called at the house, raised his hat to show dark curly hair and said to Granny that he had had a message to say Miss Downes wanted a tooth extracting.

"I'm not having a lad like you taking out my lass's tooth, you'd best send your boss," Granny said, but her daughter thought differently.

She came to the door and invited him in and had the tooth removed while sitting in a mahogany and horsehair chair which had come from the family home at Thornton.

I have the chair still, upholstered in pale green dralon.

"I'd never seen anyone with such blue eyes," she told me, "blue as the sky. Oh, he was handsome."

I wonder if she dreamed of him, but it was many years before she was to meet him again.

The years following that incident were very hard for my mother, caring for Granny and trying to keep the peace between the two ailing women. She never expected to marry. She told me, "Your granny was always ill and it took all I earned to pay for rent and food. All I got was a shilling a week pocket money, and how could I save out of that?"

There was no celebration for her twenty-first birthday and no present.

"Dr Whitely's had your present money," Granny said.

Mother did have one man friend at the time, a widower called Mr Jones who brought her flowers from his friend's allotment every Sunday morning.

"Jones was quite a nice man," she told me, "but I'd never have married him though I did like getting the flowers."

At that time her friend, Lizzie Sweeting, was walking out with a young man called Willie Taylor and one day they asked her if she would make up a foursome to go and hear a famous preacher at the church at Thornton the next Sunday.

That was how she came to meet once more the handsome dentist, though she hardly knew him, he was so changed.

He had been working away from home in Kidderminster, where he sang in the Worcester Cathedral choir. He also worked in Bournemouth and London, but ill health drove him home to his parents who lived in Springroyd Terrace, Girlington.

From childhood he had had bouts of pain and it became so bad that he had to have an operation when it was discovered he had an extra loop to his bowel, a condition which generally caused death in childhood.

The operation was successful but he developed peritonitis and hovered between life and death for several weeks. No one expected him to survive nor work again but after three months he crawled up out of bed. When he travelled by tram he was so emaciated that young women would get up to let him sit down.

Ether had been used as an anaesthetic and this had damaged his lungs, but in spite of this he managed to start work again.

It was a very fine and sunny evening on that first meeting and the other three thought it would be a good idea to go for a walk instead of going to church. Mother jerked her chin in an arrogant way when she told me this story. "I said if they wanted to go for a walk they could, but I'd come to hear a preacher and I intended to do so."

No one argued, they went to hear the preacher and afterwards the three from Allerton went off together while the dentist made his way back to Girlington alone. Mother said that when he walked away he was kicking stones angrily.

Not long after this meeting he, too, was calling on Sunday morning and soon Jones, the flower bearer, no longer came.

George Hanson was the second son of Enoch and Emily Hanson and they were a rung up the social ladder for Enoch was a salesman and traveller in the furnishing department at Lister's Mill, Bradford.

George had trained as a dental mechanic in Manningham Lane and then had gone on to become a dentist. In those days it was an apprenticeship like any other.

Now he was approaching thirty and ready to settle down, indeed it was his mother who encouraged him to do so. Perhaps she felt she had done enough for him, nursing him through that long illness.

When he came to propose Mother had to confess her shameful birth. He told her it was no fault of hers and that marriage was only a man-made law. He gave her a three stone diamond ring which must have cost quite a lot and no doubt caused a sensation and some jealousy in Allerton.

"I could never understand what your father saw in me," Mother often said. "He could have married anyone. And to hear him sing! Lovely romantic songs like 'Come into the garden, Maud.' "

I never had that pleasure for as I grew up he was singing selections like 'Trumpeter, what are you sounding now?'

The Hansons were a musical family and they would all stand round the harmonium in the little front room while Grandpa Hanson played and his family sang.

Grandma Hanson had had nine children and many miscarriages. She told my mother that she had one on a wash day and she put it in a bucket on the cellar steps while she finished the wash.

Two of her children died in a week from fever and afterwards all her hair fell out. It never grew again and for the rest of her life she wore an unchanging red-brown wig which was a great puzzle to her many grandchildren.

Annie was seventeen and Jennie fifteen when the youngest, Harry, was born. Willie (or Bill) was several years older than my father.

Grandma Hanson warned Mother, "Our George is moody."

"Oh, he won't be moody with me," Mother answered.

Her health was bad in those months of courtship and she was now working at Globe Mills in Thornton Road which meant a tram ride each day. I am not sure how she coped with a longer day for Granny had bouts of ill health when she was sometimes in bed for three months at a time living on little more than milk and water.

Mother had had a bad fall at the time and she went to see the Hanson family doctor escorted by Annie, Father's sister. For the rest of her life she had a horrible dent in her spine from that old injury.

"Your dad coming into my life just about saved my reason," she told me.

Chapter 7 "In spite of everything it was a good year."

George and Madelena (Lena) Hanson, September 1913

The wedding was planned for the 17th September 1913. Mother was twenty-three that July, my father already twenty-nine. She desperately wanted to wear a white dress and have a veil but Granny vetoed such frivolity.

"Mill lasses don't deck themselves up like that," she said, "and anyway I've no money for a white dress."

Perhaps Granny was feeling worried about her future for at first nothing was said about what was to happen.

It was Dr Whitely who reassured my father. "If you're thinking of taking the old lady to live with you, George, there's no need to worry. She won't last six months."

In June of that year a house in West Park Road became vacant and my father decided to rent it. It was detached, somewhat wedge-shaped and with a sitting room, a dining room, kitchen and two bedrooms. Best of all there was a proper bathroom with a fire-back boiler in the dining room to heat the water.

It was conveniently near Springroyd Terrace and just a tram ride from Wright Gill's surgery at Listerhills where Father worked as a dental assistant.

Mother and Granny moved into the house three months before the planned wedding leaving Hannah Maria to move to a smaller cottage. It was many years before she forgave my father for that.

Father had saved hard in the years since his operation and now he used the money to furnish the little house. They bought a three piece suite with chesterfield couch and a mahogany escritoire desk for the sitting room.

In the bedroom above there was a full suite, wardrobe, dressing table, wash stand and two single beds! This was almost unheard of in those days. There was new linoleum on the floors with rugs, and new lace and pull-on curtains at all the windows.

Granny's possessions furnished the rest of the house.

"No one could have had a nicer home," Mother often said.

What Mother would wear for her wedding was finally resolved for she had a new skirt of blue shot silk which she had worn just once, and she had a blouse made of the same material. So she had something old and new and blue, but I am not sure if she borrowed anything.

The bouquet my father bought her was certainly bridal enough, a great spray reaching almost to her feet. Not long ago a friend told me that it was said on the day of her marriage that Mother looked as dainty as a piece of Dresden china.

Granny was very smart in a dress of her favourite shiny silk. For her bridesmaids Mother had Sophie Beasley, her old friend from Allerton, and Gertie who was to marry Father's brother, Harry.

Although she no longer worked in Allerton Mother had many friends there and she arranged the time of the wedding to coincide with the lunch hour at the top mill. For in those hard times no one could afford, or even dare, to 'break time' to watch a wedding.

They were married at St Peter's Church and the reception was at the Sunday School. Mother spent the morning there arranging the tables and getting it all ready.

She had left work a few days before and she said it was the happiest day of her life to be done with the mill, the smell of wool, the dust and noise of machines which ruined the hearing of so many weavers. That rather rainy Wednesday in September must have been the second happiest day of her life.

Who, then, was to give away this fatherless bride?

The answer is in the wedding photograph, for standing behind Granny Downes, handsome and immaculate, is that old family friend and pioneer of motoring, Albert House.

The catering for the reception had been done by a shop in Allerton and as there was quite a lot of food left the bride thriftily parcelled it up and they took it with them on their honeymoon to Scarborough.

It makes me smile to think of that young couple in their wedding finery, with their suitcases and a parcel of food.

'Waste not, want not,' was their motto. In those days you paid for your room and bought your own food which the landlady cooked.

They had little money left but it was enough to go and see *The Merry Widow*. It must have seemed very different from the shows the amateurs put on in Allerton, and for the rest of her life Mother would go dreamy-eyed when she heard music from the opera.

"George and I went to that on our honeymoon," she would say. "Oh, it was lovely."

They had ten days in Scarborough so that it was the end of September when they came back to the little house in West Park Road. Winter was coming on but I doubt if they worried about that.

On Monday morning Father went to work and when he arrived at Wright Gill's house there was an empty place beside the front door. Father's sign had been taken down. He had been sacked!

No explanation was given for his dismissal. Employers could act in any high-handed way they chose and nothing could be done.

It was a terrible start to a marriage and I can well imagine Mother's terror at the thought that she might have to go back to work in the mill after such a brief escape.

"I'd have done it, too, if I'd had to," she told me. "I'd have done anything to help your father."

It was not necessary. "I'm not going to work for anyone else ever again," father said, but how he was to start was another problem for all his savings were gone.

No financial help was offered from his parents but without hesitation Granny handed over the last of her savings. Father bought a dental chair and basic equipment for surgery and workroom.

I well remember his first drill for grinding out decayed parts in teeth. It was worked with a foot pedal and for years he kept it in the corner of his surgery as a kind of museum piece.

It must have been painful for the patients and it is no wonder that people generally had their mouths 'cleared' and dentures fitted at a very early age.

They had to reorganise their lovely sitting room to make a surgery, with a screen to hide the dental equipment. The desk became a cabinet for instruments and was used for that for many years.

The dining room became the waiting room and Father turned the small cellar into a workroom.

To complicate matters Mother suspected that she was pregnant but she was soon busy learning how to become a receptionist and Father's dental nurse.

The House in West Park Road

The house was in an ideal situation, only a tram ride from both Allerton and Thornton, and the Hanson family were well known and respected in Girlington. Many of Father's patients at Wright Gill's surgery followed him to the new one.

In that first year they lived on £1 a week for Father was determined to pay Granny back as quickly as possible. Though he had grown up in a home which was higher up the social scale he had not fared so well.

He didn't talk much of the past but he remembered times when he actually went hungry, something Mother had never known. He said that when there was bacon it was always given to Grandpa and the children handed up their dry bread to be rubbed in the 'bacon dip' on the plate.

One day Mother ran down the road to buy three pennyworth of potted meat for their tea. "Can we afford that?" Father asked.

He had never had anything savoury for tea. Grandma Hanson's idea of tea was just jam and bread with stewed apple for a treat. Mother was very scornful of that. "Stewed apple! I wouldn't give you tuppence for a bucketful," she would say. "Give me a knife and fork in my hands."

Granny could make a good meal out of very little. A shillings-worth of tripe and udder with plenty of salt and vinegar made a tea for the three of them, or tripe stewed with onions made a filling dinner.

Neck of mutton was cheap, so was shin beef. I reckon my father had never eaten so well in his life before, for that failing old woman, who had barely six months to live, was now cook and housekeeper.

In the evenings while Mother and Granny sewed my father would read the works of Dickens. "He had a lovely speaking voice, like music it was, to hear him," Mother told me. "I did enjoy those readings."

Maybe Father thought he would educate his bride or maybe he just wanted to share with her what he enjoyed. He bought her the book *Jane Eyre* for Christmas and she read it many times. All her life she read constantly and I am sure those first readings started her lifelong enjoyment in literature.

The mystery of my father's dismissal was resolved some months later when his ex-boss, Wright Gill, came to see him. It seemed that money had been regularly stolen from him and he believed that only Father knew where it was kept.

Perhaps Wright Gill had heard that the house in West Park Road was being furnished in a lavish fashion, too lavish for a mere dental assistant, and had come to the wrong conclusion.

Yet after Father had been sacked the money continued to disappear and one night they came home early and discovered the dental mechanic in the house. He had let himself into the house with a key he had had made.

To quote Mother, "Wright Gill begged and prayed for your father to go back to work for him. I reckon he had lost a lot of patients, but it was the best thing that ever happened, your father being sacked and starting up on his own."

I have often wondered what Father said when he refused. It would have been polite for Father was never a swearing man.

"In spite of everything it was a good year," Mother told me many times. "I loved your dad before, but after that set-back I knew I had married a real man, a good provider, and I thanked God for it."

Chapter 8 *"Don't call me Baby!"*

The summer was a particularly hot one and Mother was now enormous and very weary. On the fourth of July my father went on a choir outing to Bolton Abbey. Granny had spent the day in bed with a 'sick headache'.

In the evening Mother walked down to Four Lane Ends to buy some tripe for Father's supper, and struggled back in pain. It was nine months and a fortnight after their wedding.

"You can't have it tonight," Granny said, "I'm too ill."

Father was late home and had to walk up from Bradford and the minute he arrived he was sent off to Allerton to fetch Dr Whitely. The doctor was in bed and Father spoke to him through the speaking tube by the front door.

"No need to panic," said the doctor, "First babies always take hours to come," and he went back to sleep.

Reassured my father tottered back home and collapsed on the couch, absolutely exhausted by his day in the sun and three long walks. He was rudely awakened by Granny a few hours later, who said, "Doctor hasn't come, you'll have to fetch him, and don't take no for an answer. And bring the nurse, too, for I'm too poorly to manage any longer."

Once more Father started the long uphill walk. In the months since his marriage he had become friendly with Dr Whitely and had occasionally gone for days out with him, but I doubt if he felt very friendly towards him that morning.

They arrived back just on six o'clock that brilliant Sunday morning but they were too late; Granny, sick as she was, had just delivered her granddaughter. Although there were no suitable scales the nurse reckoned she was between ten and eleven pounds in weight.

Much against Mother's will she was christened Alice, of blessed memory. Right from the start Granny called her all kinds of silly pet names like Mollie-moppet and Mollie Muffin-dough, and before long everyone was calling her Mollie.

Nine months before she was born Father's sister, Annie, now approaching her forties, had her last child who had been christened Margaret, but she was always called Mollie. So there was now Mollie Green and Mollie Hanson and later they were to become good friends.

Ten days after the birth Mother was back in the surgery helping Father. There was much more to do now with a baby in the house and although Granny knew a great deal about babies and had actually named the child she was never allowed to bathe her.

"Why wouldn't you let Granny bathe Mollie?" I once asked.

"She was mine, that's why. I wasn't having her taking over my baby. And your father was very fussy, wouldn't let her have anything to eat till she was nearly a year old. I was still breast feeding her and she had a full set of teeth, and fat, I've never seen such a fat baby."

Mollie was certainly fat and not particularly beautiful, and a month after she was born, on 3rd August 1914, war was declared.

"The men marching past our house used to set Mollie screaming," Mother said. She was often to hear the sound of marching feet in the years to come.

Father's younger brother, Harry, joined the army and survived the war but his wife lost two brothers and a brother-in-law in one day for they were in the locally recruited regiment, the Bradford Pals.

Uncle Willie was an engineer and much older and the next generation of the family were too young. Father was regularly called for medicals but he never passed as fit for since his operation he had suffered regularly with phlebitis.

Life had become very difficult once Mollie started walking, which happened when she was a year old, for she could climb like a monkey and could empty every drawer in the sideboard more quickly than it takes to tell.

They needed more room and yet hesitated in case the worst happened and my father was called up. Finally they decided to rent a larger house, number twenty-one, Whetley Lane.

The front of the house was very old, just a two up, two down cottage with a scullery behind, but later an addition of similar size had been built on at the back which meant there were three rooms and a kitchen.

The room to the right of the front door which had a large bay window became the surgery. The one on the left, a kind of entrance hall, was the waiting room and from this room a stone staircase led upstairs. Behind the surgery was the old scullery which was narrow and dark with a window looking to the kitchen.

Granny took one look at it and said, "It's nobbut a pigeon 'ole," and 'pidgey' it was always called. It was a useful area where buckets of coal were kept, and dental supplies. From the pidgey was a door leading to the cellar.

Upstairs were three bedrooms and a bathroom but one room had to be used for a workroom. Our kitchen was small and the living room, also with a bay, was sadly overcrowded with three piece suite, sideboard, piano, drop-leaf table and chairs.

For as long as we lived there Mother was always trying to re-arrange the furniture to make more room, an impossible task and one which annoyed Father who would sigh loudly when he saw she had been at it again.

The back door was in this room and we had a long narrow garden which led into Kensington Street. There was the usual midden there and an outside toilet and a small building which in those early days was let off as a milliner's shop. Later when Father bought the house it was changed into a garage.

I was born in the big back bedroom of this house in March 1920. It was a Friday afternoon and Mother was already up there eating her tea when she had this urgent summons. A nurse was already installed but Father was sent out to catch the tram to Allerton to fetch Dr Whitely.

Unfortunately the mills were 'losing' and every tram went past him full. By the time the Doctor arrived, this time by motor car, I was born.

Possibly Granny resented the presence of a trained nurse whom she disliked, or perhaps she resented that she had nothing to do with the birth, but it was some time in the evening when she decided to visit Mother to see her new granddaughter.

It was a cold night and the nurse had made up the fire and Granny took one look at it and said, "That fire's fit to roast a pig," and walked out of the room slamming the door.

She didn't go near me, nor have anything to do with Mother until the nurse left. As Mother said, "It wasn't my fault, I hadn't made up the fire."

It seemed I was something of a failure from the start for it had been planned that my name would be Walter and I would become a dentist like my father. Not that he even hinted at the truth.

I clearly remember the day Mother said, "It was a great disappointment to your father when you were born, but I was glad, I like girls best."

I never remember Father holding me or cuddling me, but that was partly my fault. "You wouldn't have anything to do with your father as a baby," Mother would say, almost triumphantly. I think it suited her very well for she had lacked love from her own mother and needed to be first.

Not only was I the wrong sex but from the start I caused a great deal of worry and trouble for I spent the first four years of my life either going down with bronchitis or struggling up out of it. Mother 'fell out' with a friend from Allerton who called to see us with a cold and passed it on to me the Christmas after I was born.

"She was three months without being dressed after that," Mother told someone and another time I remember the note almost of triumph in her voice when she told someone else, "This child had double pneumonia three times before she was four."

It always seemed to me that double pneumonia must be very superior to ordinary single pneumonia. "And how I kept this child alive I just do not know," she would add regularly.

Sometimes I wonder how I kept myself alive for Mother's idea of nursing bronchitis was to keep me flat on my back in bed in a room with sealed windows and a coal fire.

If I moved she would say, "Put your hands back in bed, baby."

"Don't call me baby!" I would snap back.

I hated that, and I hated being in bed and shut away in that bedroom so far away from family life. It was a very draughty house with the back door straight into the living room and the front door being constantly opened.

Mollie and Joyce

In spite of that I believe I would have recovered more quickly if I had been allowed to sit downstairs. I never remember Mollie spending any time in my bedroom, it was generally Granny who was my companion, telling me stories about life at top't hill. Talking of her brothers and sisters, of poor little Freddie and that paragon of every virtue, Alice Downes.

She would even play games with me on the days Mother decreed that I was fit to sit up and have my hands out for a short time.

It was a great luxury to be able to have my hands out, an even greater one to get out of my hated nightie and into my clothes again and walk about on my stick-like legs.

Chapter 9 "I'll never go to Heaven, I've told so many lies!"

Although Dr Whitely was many years older than my parents he made a friend of my father and invited him out for drives in his car. Finally Father decided that it was hardly fair to Mother to go for days out with the doctor and he decided to buy a car of his own.

Doctor Whitely did all he could to discourage him, telling him he was wasting his money, but in spite of this Father bought a two-seater with a dickey seat, a Hans. I can remember being bitterly envious of Mollie who was allowed to sit in the 'dick seat' as I called it, while I had to sit on Mother's knee in the front.

It is one of my first memories for I was only about sixteen months when it was bought, and as it was never satisfactory, Father didn't keep it long.

I suppose I was very envious of Mollie who, being six years older and rarely ill, was always out and about. She attended Whetley Lane school just up the road and had many friends in the area. There was always someone at the door asking if Alice could come out.

Her name must have been Alice on the school register though all her close friends called her Mollie. She was an extrovert, in everything. If she was in a play at school or Sunday School not only was she word perfect but she knew all the other parts.

She had a flaring temper, her dark eyes would flash and she would stamp both feet. The Whetley Lane area was riddled with old mine workings and Mother would say, "Don't stamp your feet or you'll go straight through to the mine."

It didn't occur to us at the time that we would only go through to the cellar if the floor did give way.

Dr Whitely was very fond of Mollie and he would sometimes take her out on his rounds and I remember she went to stay at Ripponden with his family. Mollie always made a great fuss of him, when he called.

He seemed to be a lonely man and the only love in his life as far as we knew was his little bitch, Peggy, a small tail-less black dog, a schipperke from Belgium where they were used to guard the barges.

When Peggy was guarding his car no one dare go near it and she could be a snappy little thing yet Mollie loved her, and Peggy would dance and twist her little body in ecstacy for her master.

I really disliked the doctor for though my own father was a heavy smoker of cigarettes, Doctor smoked a foul old pipe which made me feel quite sick when he came close to me.

"Go away, you smell," I remember saying to him. He was fat, too, and I hated fat men. Yet I had a great deal to thank him for because one February night,

The Girlington Area 1934

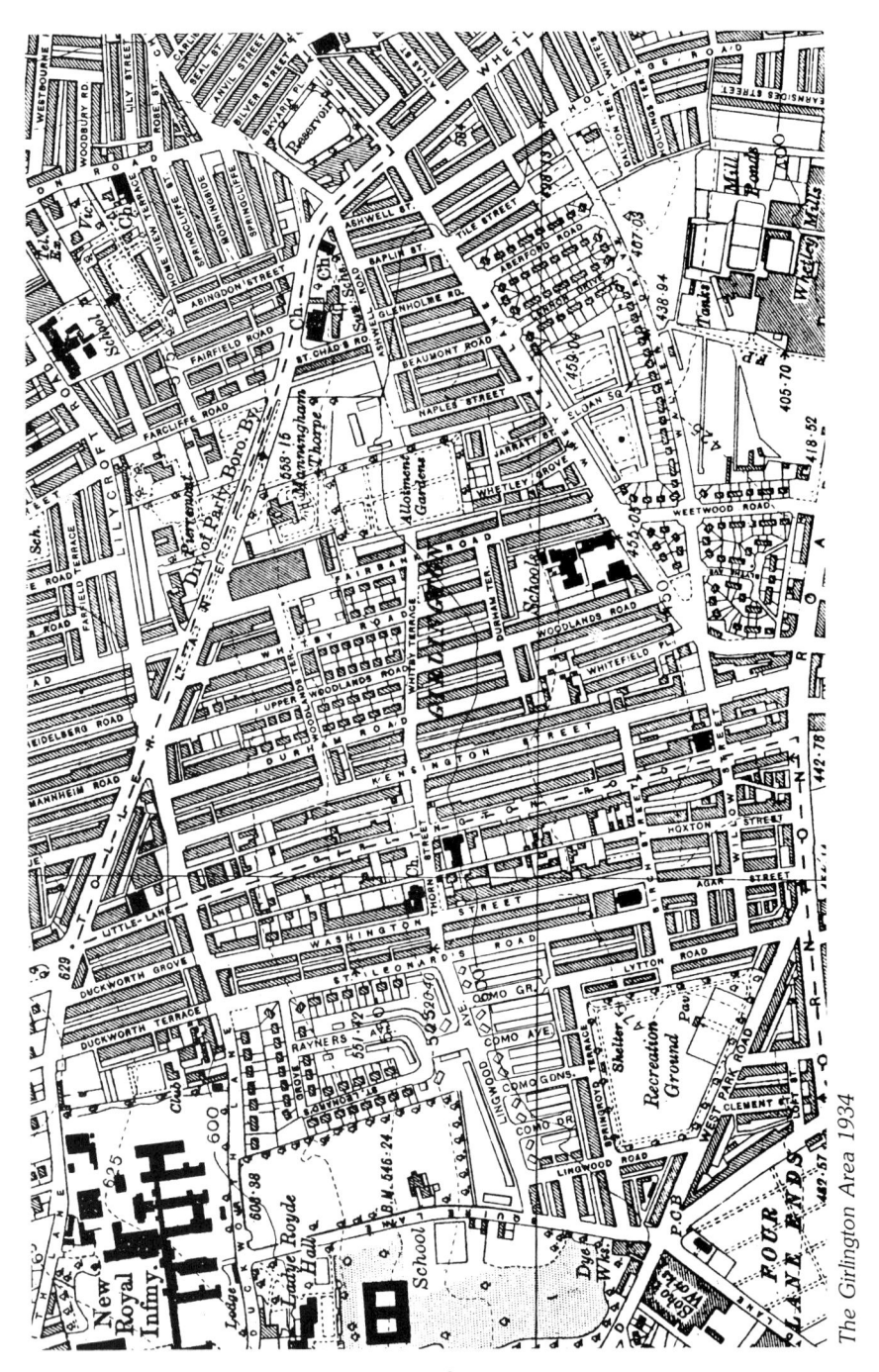

a month before I was four, pneumonia had reached crisis point and this time the doctor knew what to do.

He contacted Richard Eurich, a clever surgeon of German parentage, who was at the hospital ball that night. I remember little of what happened except being put on a table and fighting as a mask was pressed over my face.

The operation was a last hope for it entailed removing two ribs to put in tubes to drain the lung. The condition was called empyema and King George V had the same operation a few weeks after mine.

I woke in Dr Basil Hall's nursing home in Eldon Place. He was a fat man, too, but with a cheerful smiling face and he came to see me every morning to draw a family of rabbits for me. He married Norah Blaney, the actress.

Mother told me she came every day and stayed each evening until I went to sleep, often going home as late as eleven o'clock. I remember nothing of that, or of pain or fear, only Basil Hall and the rabbits.

Meanwhile Granny was at home, caring for Mollie, cooking the meals and answering the door, keeping life normal and the home fires burning. In those days there were fires in living room, surgery, waiting room and workroom, and not far away mill chimneys belched out acrid fumes.

Layers of soot lay over everything and the lace and pull-on curtains had to be washed often, and so had clothes and hands. It was a good thing we had Mother Moore.

I always called her that and never remember a time she was not at our house, cleaning and washing, helping any way she was needed, a fragile little widow who had brought up our George, our 'erbert and our Elsie, alone.

Her husband had been a driver of a brewer's dray and in those days they were paid partly in kind. Sometimes he arrived home having drunk the rest of his wages.

He had been killed falling between dray and horses and there had been no compensation and no pension for his widow. She had kept her home together by going out cleaning sometimes for as little as one and sixpence a day (7½p).

Monday morning was always washday and we had mountains of it for Father wore thick white coats, sometimes four in one week. Each patient had a linen napkin under the chin and the blood-stained ones would be soaked in cold water and disinfectant and later boiled then rinsed, scrubbed and rinsed again then starched, dried and ironed.

There were white sheets from the five single beds, tablecloths, dresses, blouses, shirts, pinafores and towels. We had a washer with a handle which you turned to 'poss' the clothes, a boiler, washboard and wooden mangle.

From nine in the morning until three or four in the afternoon there would be the thrubb-thrubb of the washboard and the drumming of the mangle. I can still remember Mother Moore's poor wrinkled hands as she ate her tea before going home.

Monday was always cold meat day but Granny generally produced something she called smothered potatoes which were sliced potatoes cooked in the big iron frying pan. I have never managed to make any potatoes so soft and tasty on the top and crispy underneath.

It was rice pudding day, too, which Father enjoyed but Mother would glance at the dish of creamy rice with the lovely brown skin and say, "Wouldn't give you tuppence for a bucketful."

Mother must have had one of the first electric irons and she spent most of Monday ironing while Granny pegged out the washing or, on wet days, dried it round the living room fire. I remember seeing her surrounded by clouds of steam rearranging the washing and then folding and handing it to Mother to iron.

Granny always called the clothes horse the winter-'edge and the rack we had above the cooker in the kitchen, the broadflake. This was pulled up high to the ceiling with a rope.

Mother would iron every inch of every white coat, sheet or towel, and then she would go the Prince's Theatre, second house, on Monday evening. She always sat in the aisle seat in the first row for she was deaf from her years of working in the mill.

She knew all the 'rep' players by name, for she was a great hero-worshipper of both royalty and stage stars. Sybil Thorndyke was her particular favourite and she took me to see her in St Joan. I also went with her to see Gracie Fields in *Mister Town of London*. Mother adored Gracie and constantly played her records, much to Father's annoyance.

He could not stand Gracie, he thought her common and so Granny always sided with him. "Ruined a good voice with her daft songs," she would say.

Father preferred classical music. I must have been tiny when he bought his first wireless with a cat's whisker. He lifted me onto the couch and I stood there leaning against the low back while he fitted great earphones over my head.

He had a pair on his head and was listening and smiling at me, as if amazed by the experience, and I smiled back though I couldn't hear a thing. He had forgotten to switch mine on but I was too shy to admit that I could not hear.

Father worked long hours for in those hard times no one could afford to stay away from work to visit the dentist and so the waiting room was often crammed with people up to eight o'clock each evening.

I hated going through the waiting room to go upstairs for they would all stare at me and there would be perhaps someone with a swollen face who had at last plucked up courage to have the tooth out.

In those days cocaine was injected as a pain killer. There always seemed to be the smell of blood which came from those awful buckets of stained cloths.

During the day Father had appointment patients but in the twenties when there was a great deal of unemployment he would sit around in the living room with little to do.

It was a restricted life he lived, working and existing in that cramped house and I believe he could have worked until midnight for after all the lights were out people would be ringing the front door bell.

"I'll never go to Heaven I've told so many lies," Mother said once when she came back from answering the door. "I said you weren't in."

Possibly because of this problem most nights he would come out of the surgery, hang his white coat in the pidgey, put on jacket, overcoat and trilby hat and walk the narrow area between front of sideboard and back of couch to the back door and across Kensington Street to the Liberal Club.

Beer did not agree with him but he enjoyed a small glass of sherry and a game of billiards before bedtime.

I wonder if Mother ever thought of that first year of marriage when he had read aloud to her while she sewed. Those days were gone and no doubt he was glad to escape from his world of women to the company of men.

Chapter 10 *"She was always there."*

Long before I went to school I spent time in the workroom with Mr Duncan, the dental mechanic, and I knew the process of denture making before I was five. He did all the basic work but Father did the 'setting up', that is fitting the teeth to the wax base which was made from the impression of the patient's gums.

I used to watch my father placing each tooth by melting the wax with a little instrument at the bunsen burner. He would take this and tilt a tooth or maybe leave a small gap between the middle teeth in an effort to make the denture look like real teeth.

He always preferred to use creamy shaded teeth but often patients who had suffered decayed teeth preferred two rows of brilliant replacements.

When the teeth were 'set up' the patient would be recalled for a 'try in' and then the actual plate would be made from vulcanite. The vulcaniser made a great hissing sound as the steam escaped, and there was plenty of dust flying about the workroom.

It was not a healthy environment for a child with a weak chest but so long as I watched quietly and didn't get in the way I was free to stay.

Soon after my operation Father had a bad attack of influenza and could not smoke and from then on he stopped, and not only did he get rid of his smoker's cough but he started me on the road to better health.

Instead he ate sweets and bags of nuts which didn't do his teeth much good but no longer polluted the atmosphere. It was many years later that I discovered I was badly allergic to cigarette smoke.

I never remember Mollie being in the workroom, she was generally playing out. Certainly there was little room for anyone to play in our overcrowded living room.

There was a great deal going on in Girlington. The public library was just across the road in Kensington Street and before school days I remember going across there with Mother and Mollie to choose books.

On the corner of Willow Street and Girlington Road was Chapman's. Mr was the barber and Mrs a hairdresser where we went to have our hair cut short in a fringe. I well remember the day when Mother took the plunge and came back home defiantly cropped and with her long plait wrapped in tissue paper.

There was a stormy scene when Father saw her and much clicking of tongue by Granny. 'Yond, as she called her, up to her tricks again.

In Girlington Road there was the fish and chip shop and sometimes for a treat Mollie would take me to buy a 'pennorth' with lots of salt and vinegar. I never remember having them as a main course at home, though two pence bought a fish in those days.

We always had fish on Friday because Granny was high church, but that came from Fitzpatricks on the corner of Whetley Lane. On Wednesdays Granny often served lambs fry; kidney, liver and sweetbread swimming in thick brown gravy. Sometimes I would go with Granny to buy hot meat pies in Girlington Road and would carefully carry a jug of hot gravy for her.

One other pre-school memory is when Uncle Harry Hanson married Louie Milnes who lived at Kensington House in Willow Street. Later it was bought for a convent.

Uncle Harry's first wife had died of the dreaded consumption in the early twenties. I remember we had new dresses for the wedding and when I saw Father at the altar with Uncle Harry I asked, "What's Daddy doing there?"

Granny went to watch the wedding but she was not invited. My grandparents never seemed to know each other well and to the end of their lives the two grandmas called each other Mrs Hanson and Mrs Downes.

By the time I reached school age Mollie was at Thornton Grammar School and though my health had improved it was decided that the rough and tumble of the board school was not for me.

A friend of my grown up cousins, Winnie Riley, had just started a private school in her father's house at the top of Girlington Road. She had called it *Netherleigh*, the title of a novel written by her uncle, Willie Riley. My parents decided to send me there.

By then Father had a Morris Cowley open tourer and at first he drove me up each morning. As winter came on it was decided that it was too far for me to go home for dinner and that I must have my meal with the Rileys.

The first day I had to stay I cried to go home and Miss Riley, very angrily, walked me home. It happened to be the day that the old kitchen range was being taken out of the living room and all the furniture was covered in dust sheets.

Mother was somewhat sooty, as was everything else, and less than pleased to see me, but Granny took me into the kitchen, soothed me and gave me some food and then walked me back to school.

After Granny's cooking I hated Mrs Riley's and I can still recall that sourish smell of boiled cabbage hanging about the house.

Like it or not, I had to put up with it, but for the rest I enjoyed school.

At the end of school we would sing a hymn and one I remember was, *The day Thou gavest Lord has ended, The darkness falls at Thy behest ...*

I used to shiver with fright, afraid that darkness would fall before I could get home. Then I would go out of school and see Granny waiting at the crossing and I knew that as long as I held her hand I would be quite safe even if darkness did fall.

Mother never met me from school and I envied the children whose mothers were waiting, and I envied them living in the terrace houses in Saltburn Terrace or Toller Lane, where they had a front and back room.

They could play together after school and at weekends while I was too far away down in Girlington.

That summer we had a holiday in Rhyl and my parents hired three-wheeler bikes for us so that we spent a great deal of time peddling around the ornamental flower beds along the front. It was a quiet little seaside town in those days, and when I got home I desperately wanted a three-wheeler bike but it was pointed out that there was nowhere in Girlington where I could ride.

Granny never came away on holiday with us but sometimes she would go away to Southport with a friend in September.

Father took one week holiday and for the rest of the summer I tended to tag on after Mollie and her friends and on the whole they were very good to me.

They used to make up shows which they acted out in the garage and I remember a popular song at that time they would always be singing. I can still remember some of the words,

> I'm the sheik of Araby, your love belongs to me,
> Each night when you're asleep, into your tent I'll creep.
> The stars from up above will guide our way to love ....

I seem to remember Mollie dressed up as the Sheik in an old sheet and with a tea towel round her head for a turban.

Mollie was always ahead of me. She taught me to charleston and she tried to teach Mother but didn't get very far for as well as being tone deaf she had no natural sense of rhythm.

Granny would sit in her chair, rocking away, watching all the tom-foolery as she called it. Father used to sigh at times; I think he was actually a man's man and resented being surrounded by females.

He took up golf around that time and used to play sometimes on Wednesday afternoon, his half day. He was a great hobby man, bridge, chess, photography, stamp collecting. Sometimes he would take us swimming but Mother would never join in.

It was Mother's proud boast that she had never been in cold water in her life and she didn't intend to start. Even when we were on the beach she would always be huddled up in a coat.

The highlight of my week was comic day. Mother and Father had no silly ideas about comics being bad for children and on holiday Tuesdays I would go and collect *Rainbow* from Mr Cowgill's shop in Whetley Lane.

Other times he would deliver it with the *Telegraph and Argus*. He had a comical way of walking, a slow shuffle which would turn into a kind of trot as he tried to put on speed.

Mother explained that he had been injured in the war and it was probably an injury which saved his life.

When Mother and Father first moved to Whetley Lane there had been a bowling green on the land opposite, but I only remember it as a kind of junk yard with a broken-down fence all round. We used to get a plague of fleas from all the rubbish and they were very pleased when the council built corporation houses on the land.

After I started school I didn't have bronchitis again. Perhaps the operation had done the trick, or the fact that Father stopped smoking. Or maybe it was that the walk to and from school each day expanded my lungs, and the Duckworth Lane area was not so polluted as Girlington.

Mother continued to coddle me and made me wear dreadful flannel bodices, with sleeves, over my liberty bodice. One day I left this awful garment off as the weather had turned warm, but Mother followed me to school and made me put it on in the Riley's bathroom.

She never bothered to muffle up Mollie like that. "I don't have to worry about Mollie, she's strong," she would say.

Mollie was strong-willed too and would not have stood for it. She was very cheeky and would answer back, even to Father. She had all the spirit and go that had been left out of me.

It was hard to follow a sister who was good at everything and popular, yet I loved her devotedly. It never occurred to me to be jealous of her, I just wished to be like her.

She was, however, a great tease and delighted in frightening me, like the time she told me that the end of the world was coming any minute. I remember rushing home, crying, up the path and into the house, terrified that it would end before I got to the safe haven of home.

"Nay, Mollie," Granny said, shaking her head, as she took me on her knee to comfort me. I never remember Granny kissing me or showing any affection, but she was always there.

Chapter 11 **Mollie**

Dr Whitely as John Bull

The year I was six I had a bad attack of whooping cough and Dr Whitely said I needed sea air, lots of it, so it was decided that Mother would rent a flat and spend the summer holidays at Morecambe.

Mother always considered she was indispensable but that summer they coped without her. Granny was there to cook the meals and answer the door, Mrs Moore cleaned and Mr Duncan would help out in the surgery when needed.

Mother always grumbled about the way Mrs Moore did the dusting for it wasn't the way Mother thought best, but that summer she could dust any old way she liked.

I don't remember it ever raining though I am sure it must have done sometimes. We were out early every morning, sometimes walking along the cliff top to Heysham, buying shrimps and sometimes even oysters which Mother said were good for me.

She was a great 'picker up of unconsidered trifles' and we spent some time mooching round antique shops and the market. In the first week she bought season tickets for West End pier and some days we would watch the show morning, afternoon and evening.

I loved the Pierrots in their shiny costumes for the opening number and though they changed the programme regularly we soon knew all the jokes and songs.

They seemed from another world and I was sure the light comedian and the soubrette were in love as they sang and danced together. I imagined there were neat little rooms behind the stage where they all lived.

Soon they knew us as well as we knew them and they would call out to Mollie and she would answer back and the audience loved it, but I would lower my head in embarrassment.

Mother loved the shows as much as we did. She could laugh as loudly as she wanted with no husband to say, "Really, Lena!" and no Granny to call her 'yond and accuse her of being extravagant.

We had her completely to ourselves and she had us. We were just three girls together and I'm glad she had those six weeks.

The worst part for me was on Sunday evening when Father had to leave us to go back to Bradford and I could never eat my tea for dread of the moment when I had to kiss him goodbye.

There was not much to do in Morecambe on Sunday evening so we usually went to church to take my mind off my trouble. One evening we were walking back while I brooded, head down, on the thought that Father would now be back in dirty old Whetley Lane.

As we passed a row of small terrace houses a man was standing at the gate smoking a pipe. He had no collar on, just a neck band and stud. He grinned at us. "Well, if it isn't Mollie," he said.

I stared and then I knew him well enough. He was the comedian from the pier, just an ordinary man living in a very ordinary house. I was utterly disillusioned, though I doubt if I knew the meaning of the word, and the magic of those shows was lost forever.

Father spent his week's holiday at Bowling Tide when all the mills closed down, then it was home again and I was glad of it, to Granny and Mother Moore and Tiddles, our tabby cat, who had pitched battles on the garden wall with Mr Cook's black tom.

Everything was ordinary again except that somewhere in those six weeks at Morecambe I had lost my whoop, I was cured.

That summer there had been a nine days wonder in Allerton. Dr Whitely, at fifty-six, was to retire and what was even more amazing, he very secretly married Mrs Lightfoot, his housekeeper.

He had a house built in St Annes and went off there taking Nellie, the new Mrs Whitely's grown up daughter, with them. I remember Mollie crying when they went, but I didn't care for there was to be a new young doctor in his place.

That September Granny had her usual holiday in Southport and Mother decided she would rent a bedroom for Granny next door but one, at Mr and Mrs Dumville's house.

I can remember it all quite clearly, packing all Granny's things and carrying them the back way, down our long garden, through the big gate that led to the back yard and the group of three houses.

The front way would have been quicker for we had small front gardens but it didn't seem right to carry piles of clothing in Whetley Lane.

Childlike I was excited by the change and particularly pleased to be a big girl sharing a room with Mollie.

When Granny came back from her holiday she cried and cried, said she was being turned out of her home, wished she was dead and gone. I cried with her for I felt guilty that I was now sleeping in her bed.

Number nineteen had no bathroom, just a lavatory in the back yard, and her daughter's action must have seemed like a betrayal after all Granny had done for us. She still spent all her days with us and only went to her new room to sleep.

Long afterwards I asked Mother why she hadn't discussed it first with Granny, or why couldn't Granny and Mollie and I have shared the bigger back bedroom.

She said sullenly, "If your dad had done what I wanted years before and had built a workroom behind the garage we'd have had three bedrooms."

Christmas was my favourite holiday for it was the one time we stayed at home. The surgery was in darkness and there were no sinister buckets of napkins waiting to be washed and no patients sitting round the waiting room.

We always had a big party on Christmas Eve and Mother had the table carried through to the waiting room. There was always a goose and a turkey, and I can remember Father and my uncles standing round the piano singing all our favourite songs.

That Christmas morning I remember standing in our big bay window in the living room playing with a toy sewing machine Santa Claus had left me. I looked up and there was Uncle Tom coming up the path.

He was married to Auntie Sophie who had been Mother's bridesmaid and, though he wasn't a real relation, I loved him very much, for he was always cracking simple jokes that a child could understand.

I clearly remember the smell of food, of my father there in the room opening a bottle of sherry and a bottle of port, and racing to the door to welcome Uncle Tom. The sun was shining, too, for a bonus.

It was my best Christmas and one I have never forgotten.

After Christmas it always seemed worse with the decorations down and the patients sitting around. I would be seven in March, Mollie thirteen in July. We were growing bigger and the living room seemed to be growing smaller.

Mollie had spent some time painting a picture for a competition in a newspaper and she was very proud of it and no doubt slightly arrogant. I remember standing in the narrow area between the back of the couch and the front of the sideboard.

I do not remember what our quarrel was about but I lost my temper, snatched her painting and tore it across. Immediately afterwards I was sorry but I don't remember apologising.

Mollie cried hysterically. She was highly strung, terrified of thunder and lightening, either up in the air or down in the dumps and that day it was definitely the dumps.

All Mother said was, "Well you can paint another one."

Poor Mollie, I was a little brute.

The January term started and Mr Beaton, the headmaster at Thornton Grammar School, was worried because there was a smallpox epidemic and he suggested that all the children in school should be vaccinated.

Father had never like the idea of vaccination and we had not been done as babies but Mollie was so scared of getting smallpox that he agreed.

The doctor came to vaccinate Mollie in Father's surgery and she chose to be done on her leg. I remember she complained that someone had slammed a satchel against it and it was very painful.

A week or so later Father went down with a bout of phlebitis and had to stay in bed and so when Mollie became really ill it was Mother who had to arrange for her to see a specialist.

I saw her being taken to the nursing home to be 'made better' but she was not my Mollie, just muttering and unconscious, for she had meningitis.

Two days later a family friend called to see if I would like to have a little holiday at her house. I was there three days and when I went home I learned the truth, Mollie was dead.

It was a month off my seventh birthday.

"Who'll play with me and take me to Sunday School?" I said through my tears.

"There'll still be Alta and Mollie Green," Mother consoled.

Alta had been Mollie's best friend but she never came to visit us again, nor did Mollie Green who had been in the isolation hospital at the time of Mollie's death and who had heard of it from another child.

All joy had gone from our home. Mollie's bed was empty and Granny moved into it. Mollie had been great at singing all the popular songs, she had been up to everything. Now there was nothing.

Our lives were split in two, before Mollie — after Mollie.

Mother clothed herself in deepest black, even to her stockings and stayed like that for years. She was not yet thirty-seven but her dark hair turned grey.

Father had dragged himself from bed to go to Mollie's funeral and looking at him someone had muttered, "Seems hardly worth filling in the grave."

Years later he said to me, "I should never have consented to vaccination, but what if she had got smallpox." I felt guilty too, remembering the torn up painting. How I wished I could go back, if only for a day, to say I was sorry.

One day I remember seeing a cloud all lined with gold and I peered up into it hoping by some miracle I would see Mollie's face smiling down at me, but there was nothing. Mollie was in the grave at Allerton and all we could do was tend the little garden there.

Someone told Mother not to be afraid to talk of her and how she talked. It was the Alice Downes situation all over again, not that she held up Mollie as an example of purity and good behaviour, rather that she was the brightest and the best. It didn't occur to me to be jealous for I had loved her, too. Life is strange. We all grow old, but Mollie has eternal youth.

Chapter 12 *"I cry a bit and pray."*

After Mollie died Mother and Father did not seem able to stay at home on Sundays and once Father got behind the car wheel he hated to stop. As Mother would never pack sandwiches we were always looking for places to eat, no easy thing in the nineteen twenties.

"There's a cafe just ahead, George," Mother would say.

"Can't stop here on the corner. There'll be another."

But there rarely was another and one time we went out for a little run and ended up at Gretna Green at four o'clock, still hungry.

Our Sunday run invariably ended at Grandpa and Grandma Hanson's house and immediately Grandpa and Father would start to argue for Father was a Liberal and Grandpa a Conservative, who had been a blackleg when Listers' workers came out on strike.

I hated and feared their outside lavatory which was a tippler, that meant a deep hole at the bottom of which was a shallow container balanced on hinges. When it became full it would tipple the contents into the drain below. It was terrifying if this happened when you were sitting there. I was always glad to get back to normal sanitation and Granny Downes.

She never came with us on our Sunday outings. Once I asked Mother why and she said, "We once took her to Bolton Abbey and she felt sick."

One Sunday afternoon I remember going in to see her in her chair rocking away and looking little and old and lonely. "What do you do all day when we're out, Granny?" I asked.

"Oh, I sing to myself a bit and I talk to myself a bit, I cry a bit and I pray." There were tears in her eyes and I knew she was thinking of Alice Downes and little Freddie and that other Alice who was always known as Mollie.

For all her life I was pulled two ways by Granny. Another time when she was sitting with her eyes closed and her mouth all drooping I went up to her and said, "How do you like my new dress, Granny?"

Her bluish-grey eyes opened wide. She put out her hand and felt the material. "What do you want with a new dress?" she said, "You've a cupboard full. You and your mother'll ruin poor George."

Granny had friends in Girlington, one was Mrs Catton and another a Mrs Mathers whom Granny always called Mrs Marrers. She had a friend, or possibly she was a relative, called Elizabeth Hannah Lord, who lived in James Street, Thornton. Sometimes Granny would stay with her but it could not have been very comfortable for Elizabeth Hannah's lavatory could only be reached by a walk up James Street, through a passage and another walk as far down.

Granny attended a little mission in Brownroyd which was very high church where the congregation called the curate "Father". I used to go with her sometimes on Sunday evenings and it always seemed strange that people, mostly old, called this young man Father.

He called to see Granny regularly and one day as he came near teatime he was prevailed upon to have high tea with us. When I got in from school there was this young man in his long black nightie-like garment sitting up to the table.

After he had enjoyed one of Mother's teas, for I don't doubt she had just 'slipped' down to the shops for some boiled ham and a box of fancies, he often called around that time.

We liked him very much and were really sorry when he moved to another church.

Although Granny made mouth-watering jam pasty, juicy mint and currant pasty and apple, too, Mother rarely ate it. Her idea of sweets for a party would be a huge trifle and dozens of cream cakes which could be bought for a shilling a dozen at Silvio's.

Father liked Granny's baking and preferred plain cake.

I still use Granny's recipe for pastry, and her method of making it. The ingredients never varied. One pound of plain flour to half a pound of lard, one ounce of butter and a little salt, and less than a quarter of a pint of cold water.

She would rub in the fat lightly with her gnarled old fingers and after adding the water would gather it gently together into a ball. She would take out about a third and roll it out, fold it in four, trim the edges. These trimmings she would incorporate into the next rolling, then tuck the last trimmings into one of the folds.

She would set aside this neat tall pile of pastry for an hour or two or often overnight.

Her steak and kidney pies were the best I ever tasted. The meat was always gently cooked the day before then put in a pie dish with par-boiled chunks of potato and topped with her crust.

It was no wonder the men had queued up at the dining rooms for their threepenny portions.

Granny treated her scone mixture exactly the same way by rolling it and then folding, then rolling out quite thinly. She always put two rounds together to bake so that her scones rose well and split easily.

I learned a great deal about cooking by just watching Granny.

We had one holiday at Morecambe after Mollie died and there is a snapshot of the three of us with Uncle Harry, Auntie Louie and little Shirley. Mother said she seemed to see Mollie at every corner and never wanted to go there again.

That Christmas we went to Blackpool leaving Granny with just a friend to keep her company. There were no other children at the hotel and I remember sitting in the crowded dining room remembering last year, with Mollie and wishing I was back at home with Granny.

I seemed to live in a world of grown-ups for I had few friends in the vicinity of home though I sometimes played with Margaret, who lived next door. Saturdays were the worst days for the bell constantly rang and patients lined up in the waiting room. Blood and disinfectant, that was the Saturday smell and I was lucky to have my swing, it was my only escape through those long boring afternoons.

Mother Moore was a good friend to me in the long holidays. Sometimes she would take me out in the afternoon when she had finished work. I went with her sometimes to 'our George's' house in Bradford Moor where I could play with her little granddaughters, Shirley and Caff. For Mother Moore could not say 'th' so it was a shame she had a grandson called 'our Kenneff'.

She was a great talker and would retell how 'our Elsie' met Fred her policeman husband. I remember Granny listening patiently while Mrs Moore told her how to make rice pudding. She thought a lot of my father. "Mr 'anson pulled my teeth," she once said, which made my Father wince for he didn't 'pull' teeth, he extracted them.

Sometimes I would go with Granny to tea at her house. She lived in Allerton Road in a back-to-back cottage which faced north. She had a sink in the cellar head, two bedrooms above and a lavatory in the yard.

If she knew we were coming she would be out watching for us, peeping down the passage into the road. If ever I went past Allerton Road on the bus I always looked up her particular passage, and even on cold days she was often there looking down towards the main road, for she could see nothing from her window but similar houses beyond the back wall.

Not long ago we drove up Allerton Road in the car and instinctively I looked up that passage as if I expected to see a small unearthly face peering towards the sunlight.

One Monday Father went into the kitchen and found Mother Moore collapsed over the washer. He brought her round and when she recovered drove her home.

"The work is too much for her now she's getting older," he said to Mother.

I remember they talked about it for some time. Mother didn't like laundries and said it wasn't right to send such soiled articles away to be washed, and finally they decided to have a demonstration of one of the new electric washing machines, a Beatty which was made in Canada.

One day I came in from school to see a strange man having tea with them, and in the kitchen was the washer, a cumbersome piece of equipment with a bench and two troughs which were for rinsing the clothes.

The whole wash had been done in about two hours and it seemed to be the answer to Mrs Moore's problems. When she heard the news the worm turned,

"If you think I'm going to use that thing you're wrong, I'll leave sooner," she said.

"Right," said Mother, "I'll do the washing and you do my Monday work."

So Mother Moore answered the door, tidied up, made the beds and 'just slipped' to the shops if necessary. "I'd no idea you did so much work on Monday morning," she told Mother.

Meanwhile Mother discovered that she just loved to wash the electric way, and later when Father was with the accountant and she was going through his balance sheet she asked, "There's nothing down here for laundry bills."

"Oh, my wife does the washing," Father said.

"In that case she should be paid. I'll put her down for £52 a year, will that suit her?"

It suited Mother very well. It was the sum of money they had lived on in that first year of marriage and it was paid each quarter into her own building society account. I remember she put my name on the account and it remained so until she died. By then it had amounted to a fair sum.

For besides this she had a dress allowance from Father for the two of us and whatever Granny might have said she was not a spendthrift.

Chapter 13 "Been to never-leave-school, 'ave yer?"

Miss Riley's school had become a flourishing concern and she decided to move to a purpose built one in Linton Drive, off Toller Lane. As this was a mile further from home Father drove me there each morning and at lunchtime I had lunch at the Riley family house.

At tea-time I had a much longer walk back to Girlington. The first part of the walk was not so bad but when I turned into Kensington Street my ordeal began. There were always quantities of little boys there and as I walked past in my maroon uniform they would jeer, "Private school kid .... " or "Been to never-leave-school, 'ave yer?"

I would walk past looking straight ahead, and terrified, and my only hope was a girl called Ethel Dufton whose father had a cobbler's shop in lower Kensington Street. About the time I was passing she would be taking her father's tea, a brimming pint of tea and a packet of sandwiches.

She went to the local school and would shout back at the boys and put out her tongue as we walked past, and I valued her friendship and admired her greatly.

For Granny no longer met me. I was a big girl now and could walk home alone.

The September after Mollie died I remember two new girls coming to school and they were brought by car each morning. Both were fair and pretty but Marian, who was about my age, had lovely waving hair and wide apart blue eyes. She was exactly as I would have chosen to be if some kind fairy had granted me a wish.

Her little sister, Irene, was just starting school and sometimes their father would give me a lift down as far as Duckworth Lane. I really liked Marian and as they also had a telephone it wasn't long before I would climb on a stool in the pidgey where ours was fixed on the wall, and ask the telephonist for her number.

Granny, who believed the telephone was an invention of the devil and would never answer it, was amazed by my great daring, and soon there were calls from Father to get off that telephone.

Exactly a year after Mollie died disaster struck, for the girls' father died. Soon after that Mother said I could invite them to tea. They lived near Manningham Park and could get a bus straight through to Whetley Lane.

It was an exciting day for me when I was invited back to their home in Selbourne Terrace. I knew they had three big sisters and a brother living at home as well as a married sister and brother, and I was amazed when I saw these older girls in their short fur coats for all three were going out when I arrived.

I didn't know it at the time but Mr Turner, their father, had been married twice, with five children by his first marriage and three daughters by the present Mrs

Turner. The house was perfect for children and young people for the basement kitchen had a full sized billiard table covered by a mahogany table top which in turn was covered by a thick green tablecloth edged with green bobbles.

We would play for hours there making tents of old dust sheets. They had a slide with a little trolley to sit on which reached from under the front window, through a door to the scullery, the full depth of the house.

Soon we were spending every Saturday afternoon together. On fine days we would play in Manningham Park, up and down the steps by the conservatory, round the lake, in Cartwright Hall.

Marian's friendship helped to heal the loss of Mollie.

After Mollie died we never had another Christmas at home while we lived at Whetley Lane, but spent them at St Annes with Dr and Mrs Whitely.

I never felt particularly happy or wanted there and was always glad to get home to Granny. Marian, too, had a grudge against Christmas for her birthday was 17th December and she usually got a combined birthday and Christmas present. As her younger sister got the same present and then had another for her birthday Marian felt she missed out.

Marian was three months older than I and so she sat for her scholarship the year before and left school to go to Belle Vue. I missed her badly but we still had our weekends together.

Around that time there was the great pageant in Peel Park in Bradford and through school Marian got into the crowd scenes. I really envied her that experience and would have loved to be in it, too, but Father would never have allowed it.

Marian was a brownie and then a guide in a company attached to her local church and though I desperately wanted to join Father would not allow it. "You might want to go camping and I'm not having that," he said.

I don't know if he thought that pneumonia would be lurking to catch an unwary camper but it didn't make sense to me for I was perfectly healthy and rarely got a cough even after a head cold.

If only Mollie had lived! I am quite sure she would have insisted on going camping, but Mollie was no longer there to open doors for me and I didn't seem to be able to open them for myself.

Time still hung heavily for me in the holidays, for our holidays rarely coincided, and Marian and her family usually had a fortnight at Cayton Bay where they lived in an old railway carriage by the beach. How I envied her those holidays with her family.

What I most hated about the summer was that Father had developed a sneaky way of filling in time between appointments by saying, "Just come into the surgery and I'll see if anything needs doing."

Usually something did need doing and once my mouth was filled with cotton wool he would lecture me on dental hygiene. "You won't have a tooth in your

Enoch and Emily Hanson, grandparents

head by the time you're twenty the way you're going," he would say.

It never seemed to occur to him that it was partly his fault for since he had given up smoking he ate sweets continually and each weekend he gave Mother a ten shilling note to spend. When you consider that a tuppeny bar of chocolate was a great solid wedge and really high class sweets did not cost much more than a shilling a quarter, we always had a large supply in the house.

Father's obsession with my teeth became a holiday nightmare and I tried to keep out of the house as much as possible. If ever he looked at me my heart would begin to race and I was beginning to almost dislike him.

It was a shame really for he had no idea I felt this way. When he decided to cap one of my back teeth with gold I didn't protest and bore the uncomfortable sessions in the chair without complaint. He was always going to the Leeds Medical School for lectures and was well ahead of his time in such work.

It seemed we were to have another dentist in the family for Father's elder sister, Annie, had a son at medical school. He had been christened Arthur Hanson Green which seemed almost prophetic.

When the time came for me to change schools Father did not want me to follow Mollie to Thornton Grammar School so it was decided I would sit the entrance examination to Bradford Girls' Grammar School. I was offered an assisted place but when the form came asking Father to divulge his income he flung it across the table angrily. "I'll pay full fees," he said.

To get to school I had to take a tram to Sunbridge Road, get off at a seedy area where the first corporation flats had been built in Bradford, walk through to Westgate, and so down Hallfield Road.

Each day I passed the window of the room where I had slept after my operation, now incorporated into the Eye and Ear Hospital. Life at the new school was interesting and exciting and soon I made friends with a girl called Joan Coventry. She was tall and well made.

"I thought you were an awful stupid giggling little thing," she said once, looking down at me from her superior height. "You see I was so very shy."

I was shy, too, but had learnt to hide it thanks to Marian and her family. Joan's parents were southerners and she spoke with the long a. Actually I never called her Joan, everyone called her Covie.

My trouble there was that I felt different from the other girls, as I had felt different at Netherleigh, coming as I did from what was the edge of a slum. At home I was the only Grammar School girl for miles. One day I was with a group of children in the back street and I heard someone mutter, "She goes to the Grammar School."

"She never," said another child as if utterly shocked by this revelation, and they all turned to stare at me as a herd of cattle might stare at a strange dog in their field.

I did not stay regularly to school dinner but when I did I really enjoyed it. The dining room was looking onto Manningham Lane and I only remember one menu, beef or cottage pie. I always chose beef for it was really delicious, cut from a huge joint.

To follow we had steamed or baked pudding with custard and in case we were not completely satisfied this was followed by great dishes of rice pudding. We kept our spoons and passed up our plates for this and following our plate would be the chant, "Skin" or "No skin", according to the wishes of the owner of the plate.

I chose to play hockey rather than netball because Mollie had played hockey. We played at Lady Royd in Squire Lane, where the junior school was, and we had to take hockey sticks and pads with us, also our cases of books for that night's homework.

After hockey I had to walk back to Whetley Lane with all my gear and one day when I reached the bottom of Squire Lane I was so exhausted that I decided to call at Grandpa and Grandma's for a rest.

They were just having tea and they made me sit down and have some with them and that jam and bread followed by stewed apple tasted pretty good to me.

It is the only time I remember visiting them without my parents and the only time I had tea at their house, but I remember their pleasure at seeing me and their kindness.

I can see them so clearly in memory, my tiny grandma with her neat wig, long skirts and white apron, and Grandpa with his crinkly smiling eyes and his face concealed by a greying beard.

Sometimes now as I look into the face of my son, who also has crinkly smiling eyes and a beard, I can see Grandpa's face, too.

Chapter 14 Toller Lane

For as long as I could remember Mr Duncan had worked for Father, but all I knew of him was that he came from Leeds, and after he married, his wife would not come and live in Bradford.

He was away for many weeks, ill, and in the end Father had to get another mechanic. At first Miss Craven came to help out at weekends and in the evenings but later she came full time.

The year after that my cousin, Arthur Green, qualified and it was decided that he should come and work with Father, and eventually take over at Whetley Lane and Father would open a branch surgery.

Mother and Father spent some months house hunting and eventually decided on a chalet bungalow at the top end of Toller Lane which would be big enough for the second surgery.

The house had been empty for some time and the rooms were cold and damp and the garden neglected, but from the back windows there was a wide view to Baildon Moor, Hollins Hill and to some pimple on the far horizon which was said to be the shooting box on Ilkley Moor.

The house was built into the hillside so that there was a garage and wash house in the basement, two reception rooms and kitchen and two bedrooms on the ground floor and a further two bedrooms and a boxroom upstairs.

For the first time I had a room of my own up under the eaves and I could have Marian to stay. I had long wanted a dog though we still had our old cat, Tiddles. I even had hopes of a bike but they soon squashed that notion.

Father paid a thousand guineas for the house and reckoned he had given too much for it was not well built, the windows fitted badly and naturally there was no central heating for that was considered extremely unhealthy.

There was a long drive leading down to the turn round at the back of the house which faced due north, and beyond our back fence nothing but fields between us and Heaton Woods.

As far as I know Granny was never consulted about the move and for her it was not a good one. Although her eyesight was failing she still attended church and went out to see her friends or do the shopping. At Toller Lane she was completely isolated.

Her shabby old rocking chair was put in the kitchen of the new house and Mother had the rockers taken off because she said they took up too much room. It was put at the right hand side of the Yorkist range backing onto the outer door. I am sure Granny missed the gently rocking movement but she never complained.

The kitchen was appallingly badly planned with the sink in the corner behind cupboard doors and the cooker by the back door so that if it was opened the gas jets would blow out.

Our dining room was above the garage and on windy days the carpet would rise and fall so that one had the feeling of floating. The bathroom was on the east side of the house, with no heating, so that face flannels were known to freeze in the winter.

I doubt if the fact that you could see the shooting box from the kitchen window meant much for Granny who now had to stand on the fender to look at the clock, a dangerous procedure which scorched her dress on one occasion.

It was late autumn when we moved in and my fourth term at the grammar school. That winter was the very worst for years. Snow in Girlington had been filthy stuff which was soon cleared by Mr Cook who kept the garden tidy.

There was no Mr Cook in Toller Lane and the snow was very different, sculpted in great sweeps that covered the turn round at the back and the steep north-facing drive.

For the first time in years Father had to use public transport and it was no easy journey for there was no direct bus route to the surgery.

The buses were irregular and when they did come invariably swept past full. I did enjoy the sledging, though, especially at weekends when Marian would come to stay and we would whizz down the 'bump' very near Heaton Woods.

This hill was actually in sight of an old farmhouse, now divided into two homes which was the very one where Granny's half brother, Ben Redman, had lived with his wife and the survivors of their seventeen children.

The quarry was the very same where Ben had worked as an overseer, and when the weather improved stone was still being taken out of it.

Until we moved to Toller Lane Ben had been just a vague name to me from those stories Granny used to tell of life at top't hill in Thornton. But there were still Redmans living in Heaton and soon Granny was talking again, remembering and even smiling when she recalled how her long dead half brother would play the cello in duet with her father, William, on his double bass.

For Mother the move to Toller Lane had seemed like a dream come true, a spacious home in a beautiful situation and freedom to live her own life. It didn't quite work out like that.

At Whetley Lane there had been people coming and going and there was always a chance to 'slip' out to the shops or even to town and always someone there to keep Granny company.

Now the two of them were together and alone for hours on end and they just did not get on. Mother had always been a squirrel and had lots of parcels of material put away, still wrapped up in brown paper.

Granny, when left alone, would poke through Mother's possessions to see if she had anything new in her wardrobe. " 'yond'll ruin poor George," she used to say regularly.

I remember hearing Mother say to her, "Look, Mother, you've opened this parcel three times. Take a good look at it and then leave it alone."

68

Not long before we went to live at Toller Lane the neighbouring ladies had visited each other leaving cards. They were still not very willing to welcome a newcomer and at the bus stop a reserved, "Good morning", was all the greeting given.

When Spring came Mother became friendly with our neighbour whose back door faced ours on the west side of the house. Mr and Mrs Laycock had no children but Mrs Laycock's orphan niece Sheila lived with them and as our bedrooms faced across the gap we often talked from our bedroom windows.

They had two dogs, an alsation and a schipperke bitch just like Dr Whitely's little Peggy. Sheila told me horrifying tales about how the alsation hated cats and would kill ours on sight. I was very worried, for Tiddles was getting old, but one day when we heard the alsation barking madly I opened the kitchen door to see Tiddles sitting on the dividing fence outstaring the dog.

When the schipperke came on heat she got out and mated with a brindle bull terrier and the resulting pups were far too big and she died soon after they were born. By then Tiddles had fulfilled his unfortunate name and had become very dirty and had to be put down, but his loss meant we could have one of the pups which looked very like labradors. We called him Teddy and he was adored by us all, especially by Granny.

Father's plans for a surgery at Toller Lane never materialised. Perhaps if he had fitted it out immediately when Arthur joined the practice and left him at Whetley Lane there would have been a better chance of success.

The patients were wary of the new young dentist and probably there were other problems which I never knew about for very little was said at the time. Father had worked alone for a long time and I am sure he would not be easy to get on with.

Finally Arthur found another post in Leeds and stayed there until he joined the army during the war. When Father retired at the end of the war Arthur took over the practise.

After Arthur left, Father must have had a hard time, for he had no receptionist nor help in the surgery except when Miss Craven came down to help with gas cases. More often though he had a qualified doctor in when he extracted teeth by anaesthetic.

By then he finished work at six and came straight home, though he still worked on Saturday until five o'clock. He no longer wanted to drive around the countryside but stayed in his garden or took Teddy for walks in Heaton Woods or round Six Days Only.

I have a feeling that Mother missed her days out and there was an edginess in their relationship which I had not noticed before. They would argue about the most trivial subjects, which way a joint should be carved, with the grain or against; or which way a piece of coal should be put on the fire.

From just such trivial beginnings a quarrel would develop and my father would go into what Mother called 'a cloud', barely speaking to any of us.

I often remembered then what Granny Hanson had said when they were married. "Our George is moody."

He was moody, but no doubt in pain a lot of the time from his veiny legs. He liked to be quiet.

I believe Father would have been happy with a life of study. He read philosophy, was intrigued by the theory of time and read widely on that subject. All the time he was questioning, searching and researching. He read the Bible constantly, and poetry.

Granny admired him and always took his part in any argument. She would shake her head with wonder at his wide knowledge.

She used to say, "George has a book that tells you everything."

He had many reference books but the one Granny meant when she spoke of the 'book' was dear old *Pears Cyclopaedia*.

Chapter 15 *Granny Sitters*

We had many visitors after we moved to Toller Lane but the ones I remember most vividly were Grandpa and Grandma Hanson who came to Sunday tea to see "our George's fine new house."

For once Grandma was without her white apron but with her usual dark skirt covered with a warm coat and on her head a bonnet tightly fastened over her wig.

It was only then I realised how blind Grandpa was getting for he was trying to hang up his hat on a hook he expected was there. Mother refused to have any hooks to spoil the oak panelling so I took his hat and led him to a chair in the drawing room.

I believe it was the only time they were well enough to come to tea and though Father went regularly to see his parents it was Uncle Harry and Auntie Louie who bore the brunt of their failing health.

Although Shirley, their daughter, is much younger than I, she remembers far more about them, for Grandpa used to call on them each day and would sometimes go to the shops for her mother.

One afternoon he was coming across West Park, known locally as 'The Rec', with a pound of butter for Auntie Louie, at the same time as the park keeper was going on his rounds locking the park gates.

When Grandpa came to a gate and found it locked he wandered on to the next which he also found locked. In the end he pushed his stick and the butter through the railings and climbed over. He would be about eighty-four at that time.

He wore green glasses outdoors for it was said he had ruined his sight as a young man reading by candlelight. Uncle Harry went each day to dress a sore on his elbow which would not heal, believed to have been caused by ill treatment while he was still at school.

Grandma had had an operation for breast cancer while she was still in her forties and was never in very good health but she would sometimes manage to walk as far as her son's house. One time when Auntie Louie was in bed after baby Margaret was born Grandma walked into the room to see her tucking into a plate of fish and chips.

She was horrified. "Fish and chips for a liggin'- i '-bed woman, she should be having gruel." Shirley remembers snuggling up to Grandma's 'sealskin coat', not really sealskin but one of the first fur fabrics made by Listers.

Grandma loved to read but thought the theatre wicked. However when staying at Morecambe she found her favourite, *Daddy Long Legs,* on at the theatre. She was persuaded to go and she loved it, though whether she ever went again to the theatre we never knew.

Knowing this now I can understand how she had little in common with Granny Downes and no doubt this was why the two old ladies never got on more than on conventional terms.

Grandpa had been something of a drinker but in later years he was a gentle and caring husband and looked after Grandma when her memory began to go. In the end they had to have a housekeeper to care for them but it was very difficult to keep anyone for very long. I remember they had two single beds at opposite corners of their little front room.

They died of pneumonia within six hours of each other so that neither knew the other had gone. It was before the days of sulphur drugs and penicillin when pneumonia was called the 'Old Folkes' Friend'. Grandpa was eighty-seven, Grandma eighty-six.

'In death not divided' was the headline in the newspaper. The date was 13th April 1934 and they had been married almost sixty-four years.

Uncle Harry could now move to a larger home with a garden yet he must have missed his parents and that daily visit.

For months afterwards whenever my father drove into Squire Lane he would automatically brake at the turning to Springroyd Terrace, then he would sigh heavily and drive on.

Mother Moore continued to work for Father and would go early in the morning to light the fires and clean the surgery. One day a week she came to work for Mother; Father would drive her up at nine o'clock and she would stay until after tea. Those afternoons Mother would go out shopping for it was becoming increasingly difficult to leave Granny alone.

Although I do not remember Mother ever talking about her relations in Heaton before we moved to Toller Lane we now made their acquaintance and they were also used as Granny sitters.

Ben Redman's three unmarried daughters lived in a cottage in Highgate, Mary the eldest who was blind, Agnes the youngest and Annie, who joined them when she was too old to continue work as a nanny.

Annie had travelled widely and had lived in India and as head nurse in large houses she had acquired a 'posh' accent. She had fascinating tales to tell of India when, with her charges, she had watched banquets from the balcony above the state dining room when members of the royal family were being entertained.

One of her charges was the illegitimate son of a royal prince and before she took the post she had to sign that she would never divulge the name of the child's father, and she never did.

I used to love to go home to find 'Cesin Ennie' as we called her, though not to her face, for she was a lovely person and now I wish I had asked her more about her past life. When I hear the song, 'Other people's babies', I always think of her.

Unfortunately Granny didn't appreciate Annie. "I don't want her," she used to say. "She talks too fine, I can't tell what she says."

Granny much preferred Ada to sit with her, she was a widow of Ben Redman, the second, and mother of Ben, the third. She had come to work in Bradford as a scullery maid and had been married from North Hall Farm.

On their wedding day they were driving up Toller Lane from the farm to go to their new home when, where the road narrowed by the old Hare and Hounds, they had backed up carts to block the road and showered them with rice and old boots.

"It would take more than a few farm carts to block it up these days," she said, her dark eyes twinkling, for she came of gipsy stock.

Ada gave me her precious Mrs Beaton Cookery Book when I was married and I have it still. I often dip into it for it makes interesting reading.

Granny sitters were badly needed now and sometimes in the evenings I was left in charge. One time when I was about fourteen Granny got up quickly, stumbled on the rug, and thought she had stood on the dog's paw.

She started to scream and would not stop though I tried to show her the rucked up rug and the dog sleeping peacefully. It was no good, she screamed on and on, holding her heart, clasping her head, quite beyond reason.

In the end I managed to undress her and get her to bed, gave her a drink and two of her pain killers. She calmed down at last and after a while lay unmoving. I kept creeping into her room quite convinced that she was dead.

I was so frightened that after a while, though it was winter, I went outside and waited for Mother and Father to come home.

Mother glanced at her sleeping parent, quite unperturbed. "She used to have them regularly when we lived with Hannah Maria," she said. "It's what she called a gird and she would fall down under the bed and I had to drag her out. She'll be all right in the morning."

Next morning Granny was sitting up in bed as usual drinking her tea and rubbing her beaker across her forehead as she always did to soothe her aching head, but I was still shaken.

Holidays now became a problem and Mother never knew for sure if she would get away until we were actually driving off, for Granny invariably became ill when she knew one was looming.

One time we were going to fly to the Channel Islands and when she was told Granny said in her clever way, "Good idea, then if you come down in the sea I won't have to bury you."

Not long after this an aeroplane came down in the sea between Jersey and Guernsey and Granny must have regretted her words for she went berserk at the idea of us going by air.

They quickly cancelled the flight and booked to go by sea although Mother hated this as she was a very bad sailor. Even this change of plan did not pacify Granny and we had a bad time until the day we set off on holiday.

Her last words were that we would all be the death of her, but when we returned she was in excellent spirits having enjoyed the company of the friend Mother had asked to stay with her.

I remember another terrible outburst of temperament the summer we went to southern Ireland, taking the car this time. She never wanted Mother to go away but would have been much happier if they had settled for Morecambe. But Morecambe was 'out'. It was years before they visited that place again where there were too many memories of Mollie.

My last years at the Grammar School were unsettling, not just for me but for the whole school because Busby's, after taking up shop after shop in the parade, now wanted the school building.

They took the corner in Hallfield Road so that we no longer had offices or dining room. The year we were studying for school certificate our form room was in a rented house in Eldon Place so that we were constantly going backwards and forwards between the two buildings.

We moved into the new school in Squire Lane in time for us to take the examination there, but I was determined to leave after that, and that September I went to Bradford Secretarial College.

Around that time there came a great change in Father's family for Eddie, Uncle Willie's only offspring, was sent to be his firm's representative in Toronto. He and Ida, his wife, with their two little boys had lived quite near us in Heights Lane and they often came to see us.

Sometimes Ida would leave the children for a short time and I remember on one occasion Granny entertaining them by rolling oranges up and down on the sitting room floor.

She really loved them and I can remember her tears when they came to say goodbye. "I'll never see them again," she said, and she never did.

I could not bear to go and see them off at the station for Canada seemed a very long way away in those days. It didn't occur to me how dreadful it was for Uncle Willie and Auntie Alice with 'our Eddie' going so far away.

After that Auntie Alice often came to visit us and Mother would never let anyone leave without the comfort of a good tea. Auntie Alice was in poor health but she did manage to visit Toronto before she died, but the little boys were young men before we saw them again.

Chapter 16 *"Those Infernal Machines!"*

When the time came to apply for a job I had hopes that I might try for one on our local paper but Father would not hear of it. Through college I was offered two jobs as a shorthand typist in an insurance company or as a machine operator in a bank.

"You'd better take the bank job," Father said, "there's a pension for women at fifty."

I laughed at that but Father didn't see it as a cause for amusement for pensions were important. He had torn up his insurance cards when he became self employed and would have to live on his savings when he came to retire.

That first day remains vividly in my mind for it was April the first, quarter end, and another girl, Cissie McLellan, was my companion.

They were far too busy to bother with us so we were sent down to the basement to file away customers' cheques, and that was no easy task for private customers did not have their names printed on the cheques and the signatures were sometimes impossible to decipher.

Before the accounting machines were installed the two secretaries had a snug little room to themselves but now they were in the same room and the machines were big and clumsy and extremely noisy.

The accounts were split alphabetically into three sections and one girl processed the cheques as they came in each day and the following morning another girl processed them onto the statements. These two sets of work had to balance, but rarely did.

We were given a few days to learn the process and then had to take on a whole section. At first I had to work all through my lunch hour and late into the afternoon to get the work done.

It was so easy to press the wrong button and make a mistake and often a whole statement had to be re-copied. My back ached, my head ached and the senior secretary's nagging about 'those infernal machines' did nothing to help.

Friday was the worst day for we had to stay late to do a third lot, the statements for that day and if we worked past seven o'clock we got half a crown (12½p) tea money. Even in those days it did not buy very much of a tea! If we worked straight through and finished just before seven we got nothing.

On Saturdays the bank closed at midday but we were lucky if we got away before half past one. For this I earned £60 a year!

The worst aspect of bank life was the year end, 31st December. In the weeks before Christmas the men would stay late several nights a week working out interest and commission on every account.

After the bank closed and the work was finished on the 31st we had to process each account while one of the men sat beside us dictating the interest and commission. We had to stay until the work was finished no matter how late it was so that we were ready to open at ten o'clock the next day.

The first of January was a working day like any other and it was only when the war came that the banks decided to close on that day so that we could catch up on the work. It was certainly no holiday for us.

The only bearable part of working in the bank were the friends I made there. Unfortunately I had lost touch with my school friend, Covie, and was not to meet up with her again until the end of the war, but there were many others to take her place.

Marian worked as a telephonist for the Post Office Telephones and she was on shift work, eight to eight in the working day, for girls did not work nights until the war came. Another good friend was Renée, who lived near and who was also at the exchange, and the three of us regularly went to dances together.

Sometimes we would walk home in the small hours along Manningham Lane to sleep at Marian's. There were so many dance halls in those days: King's Hall, Queen's Hall, the Connaught Rooms, and often on Saturdays there was a 'hop' at St Barnabas' Hall in Heaton.

Granny used to get very perturbed about my friends staying late at our house and would peer at the clock and say rather pointedly, "There's a bus at quarter past."

I remember she once looked at the hem of Renée's dress and said, "That dress is too short." Luckily my friends all knew her and never minded her remarks.

We were growing up in times of war or rumours of war. During the Spanish Civil War Marian's elder sister became very friendly with two Spanish girls who had brought to Bradford groups of refugee children.

My cousin, Miriam, had been working in Czechoslovakia and for a while ignored appeals from her parents to come home. In the end she had a warning she could not ignore and got away just in time.

Once the sight of soldier or airman in the road would be very unusual but suddenly boys we knew in the area disappeared to return on leave in uniform.

There were still plenty of boys left to dance with and sometimes I would tell Granny about my evenings out, just to cheer her up, for she was getting old and frail and spent hours sitting by the fire, either in the kitchen, or by the ingle nook in the sitting room.

She would sit waggling her foot and Father would say, "Stop waggling your foot, Granny."

She would stop only to start again in a short while. When Father could no longer stand it he would say, "Time for bed, Granny," and she would go off to her room which was the warmest in the house as it backed onto the kitchen fireplace.

Once in bed she would start to say her prayers which she now chanted aloud. She would give a great groan and say, "Oh, Lord, bless the man, the woman and the child." After this there were other people to bless and requests to be made. She had a flow of language many a non-conformist preacher would do well to imitate.

After the prayer routine she would recount stories, old and new, or go over happenings which she would embroider, for she was a born story-teller.

One night I was passing her door when I heard my name and stopped to listen. "There was this lad," she was saying, "he walked into the dance hall and saw our Joyce, then he went and took his clothes off and asked her to dance."

Father would not let me learn to drive until I was eighteen, so soon after I started to work at the bank he arranged for Mr Roper, who had a garage in Ingleby Road, to teach me to drive.

After a few lessons Uncle Tom Finnigan, Auntie Sophie's husband, was called upon to take me out and that was lots of fun for we would stop in Ilkley to buy ice cream and we generally carried on like a couple of kids.

Father was not satisfied with either teacher so he also took me out along Rhodesway and made me do three point turns until he was satisfied I had reached his exacting standard.

That September was to be their silver wedding so they decided to celebrate it early with a trip to Switzerland in June. It happened that my driving test was fixed for the week they were to be away, so it was arranged that Uncle Tom would take the car to work that day and bring it for me to take the test.

Auntie Annie, Father's elder sister, agreed to come to stay with us but naturally long before that Granny had started working herself up to her usual pre-holiday panic. No doubt it was far worse this time for Mother was going into foreign parts.

"They don't live like us," she said, shaking her head sadly.

In spite of all this Mother and Father got off safely and on that first Saturday afternoon Uncle Tom arrived to give me my last driving lesson before the test.

At that time I had a silly little toy called a toot which made a flute-like sound when it was blown. We were laughing in the hall and I blew a blast on the instrument. Granny gave a dramatic scream, saying I had frightened her and went into hysterics.

She had been sitting by the fire, yards from where I blew it, and she was deaf anyway, but there was no saying anything in justification, not with Granny clasping her heart and her head.

Immediately all attention was on her. We gave her whisky, hot tea, pain killers but she still carried on alarmingly. Auntie Annie told me to ring for the doctor.

Dr Agnes Cunningham was on duty and she said she would come immediately and meanwhile to bathe Granny's feet alternately in hot and cold water. I couldn't see how this would help but we carried out the instructions in the sitting room for Auntie Annie said she must not be moved.

When the doctor arrived we got Granny to bed where she lay like a deflated balloon, dead still. Dr Agnes took me out into the hall and asked where Father and Mother were.

"They went to Switzerland two days ago."

"I think you should send for them," she said and looked so serious that I began to panic.

It was then I remembered that winter night four years before when she had frightened me to death. A gird, Mother had called it.

"No," I said, "I won't send for them. If she dies I suppose I will have to, but not until she does." Dr Agnes must have thought me heartless but they had looked forward to their holiday for months.

Next day Granny was sitting up eating her breakfast, no worse for the 'gird' though Auntie Annie, after a bad night, looked shattered. She never came to Granny-sit again, nor did Granny ever have another 'gird'.

In spite of all the panic I passed my test quite safely and had a lovely time driving around and just to celebrate did sixty miles an hour down Thornton Road, with Marian by me, clutching the door and telling me to slow down.

Mother and Father really enjoyed their week in Lucerne followed by a week in Lugano, and a day trip to Italy where they visited Milan Cathedral.

For years afterwards Mother would start a sentence with, "When we were in Italy ..." as if she were an expert on that country.

They arrived home in the small hours of the morning. After spending a night on the train Mother wanted to stay in London but Father insisted on coming straight home.

He left Mother at the station with the luggage and walked home for the car and they were both shattered for days afterwards and barely speaking.

Some Silver Wedding trip!

Chapter 17 The topsy-turvy world of war

Most people who lived through it can remember 'the day war broke out'.

It certainly stands out in my memory for Mother and Father had their own private war and a real rip-roaring affair it was. Mother and I spent the afternoon rushing up and down stairs fixing up black-out curtains and meanwhile Father had his own plans made.

He had been going into the subject of war preparation and had bought a tin of adhesive paint which was said to prevent glass shattering and he proposed to paint each window. The snag was that it rendered the glass opaque.

Mother was just as determined that it would not be done. Father was round-shouldered from long years at the dentist chair but when he was angry he would stand up very straight.

"Watch out, he has a poker up his back," Mother would mutter, and that day the poker was very much in evidence.

Granny took no part in the battle, she sat there, eyes half closed, foot wagging for she had lived through many wars both domestic and international. Mother won that battle. He never did paint the windows.

"War or no war, Hitler isn't going to take away my view of the shooting box on Ilkley Moor," Mother said.

The next evening I drove her down to St Barnabas' Hall in Heaton, now a centre for London evacuees and she was so upset at the sight of these labelled children that she just stood there crying.

All had been fixed up with homes except for one little boy who was sitting alone and though Mother would have preferred a girl we took him home with us.

He was eight and his name was Teddy, the same name as the dog which made it difficult. He had had an unsettled life for his mother had remarried and he had spent most of his time with an aunt and uncle.

He settled in quite well and went to Daisy Hill School with the local children and to the Methodist Sunday School in Haworth Road. Mother bought him a little suit, the first he ever had, and the thrill of it rather went to his head.

Mother found it difficult having such a young child in the house, especially as Granny was growing frail so that she was somewhat relieved when Teddy's aunt and uncle decided they wanted him home again. He survived the war, as did all the family and kept in touch for many years.

Wartime banking was not easy. Mr Mead, the bank messenger, was the first to go for he was in the territorials, and gradually other men were called up and in their place girls straight from school joined the staff.

It was a topsy-turvy world. Juniors who were called up would often come back on leave with commissions. The older men were generally drafted into the ranks of the pay corps. Mr Mead came on leave as an officer with a Sam Browne belt round his ample waist, a fine figure of a man.

The Bank's Fire Watchers

We were now promoted from being machine room girls to the dizzier heights of clerking. Margaret was put on the counter, an almost unheard of honour. Cissie got a very comfortable number in charge of clothing coupons which were dispensed by the banks.

Miss Simpson, the senior typist, became supervisor of the machine room girls. I had a series of jobs, sometimes I was sent out as 'second man' to a smaller branch, a job I hated for I had had no training in general banking duties.

Eventually I was put on deposit posting which was done manually in great ledgers which had to be humped up onto the desks from slots beneath. This had originally been done by a senior man with the help of a junior.

One of my jobs was to collate all the figures from every department of the bank and balance it. People would stroll past and say, "Haven't you balanced yet?"

It never seemed to balance first time and after all these years I sometimes dream that I am adding up columns of figures and getting a different answer each time.

Sometimes cheques would be written so carelessly that in the rush of work the girl who processed the statement might make the same mistake as the girl who had processed the ledger. This meant that the two balanced but their figure did not tally with the counter figure.

Mr Long, the accountant, was a kindly and long-suffering man with a perpetual cold, and yet a talent, if you will pardon the pun, for sniffing out mistakes. I do not know how the bank would have functioned without him in those war years.

He was rarely away ill and never seemed to take a holiday yet he was very under-valued by the manager.

In those days there was a clearing house in Bradford where all the banks brought local cheques to be exchanged. It had been the junior's job to go there twice each day. Later anyone who happened to be free had to go and it was a job I hated.

First clearing generally clashed with the lunch break and though it should have been a quick transaction there was always someone who could not balance and everything had to be rechecked.

The war might be going badly but, war or no war, Clearing had to balance. So had everything else in the bank, down to the last penny.

Yet, in spite of all our problems, we had lots of laughs and I remember one day the manager creeping from his room in that sneaky way he had, staring balefully at me and saying, "You spend too much of your time laughing."

He must not have read the posters exhorting us to 'Keep Smiling'. No one could accuse him of laughing too much for in all my eight years I never saw him smile, nor do a thing to help his hard working staff.

Miss Simpson, whose desk was behind the counter partition, just across the aisle from mine, would lean over to talk. One day as the manager shuffled out of his door she said, "Just look at him, for all the world like a tortoise coming out of its shell. Know what he did the other day? Turned his back on me, put his hand down the back of his trousers and scratched his bottom!"

As the war progressed more women were taken on and some were put in charge of small sub-branches, alone except for a bank guard whose boring job it was to sit in the background in case of trouble.

In theory the bank made up the salaries of the men in the forces but pay had been so low and so many ended the war with commissions that this was rarely necessary.

Meanwhile the work was done by women and girls, relatively cheap labour. After eight years with an annual rise of just £10 I ended my career in banking with a salary which worked out at just over £3.00 a week. I believe I did get a small bonus on top of this.

Mother's main preoccupation now was keeping Granny warm. Coal was rationed and the rooms were large and draughty. We had a gas fire in the dining room but it was the coldest room in the house, above the garage and with windows to north and east.

In those days roofs were not insulated so that any heat that was generated went straight up to warm the atmosphere.

Father had a meagre ration of petrol but he was afraid to use the car for he had to keep some petrol in the tank in case he was called out to a 'bleeding case'.

In those days when the whole mouth was cleared of teeth bleeding could be excessive, and it was always the dentist's task to go and plug the sockets. As Father generally carried out these major operations on Saturday morning he was invariably called out at the weekend.

Because he could no longer get home at lunch time on certain days he would go by trolley bus to town and we would go out to lunch together, sometimes to the Mechanics Institute where there was a small restaurant. It got to be rather like a club for we would meet the same people each day.

Sometimes we were lucky and would be served a chop but more often it was some anonymous mixture shaped as a rissole. In those lunch hours I actually came to know my father better and discovered that he had a sly sense of humour.

Since we had both started working Marian and I had never managed to have a holiday together but in June 1940 we both had leave at the same time. My leave was cancelled without warning. It was the time of the Dunkirk evacuation.

A fortnight later it was decided that the staff should be given a three day holiday in turn and mine was to start the next Saturday. I decided I would go to Morecambe for I had heard that the dancing at the Winter Gardens was great for the R.A.F. had taken over the town.

Mother refused to let me go alone and quickly arranged for someone to stay with Granny and Father. That Saturday evening I went along to the Winter Gardens alone. The entrance fee was ninepence but sixpence (2½p) for servicemen. For this sum you could also see the show, Henry Hall's Guest Night.

An R.A.F. recruit came and asked me to dance. He was wearing hob-nailed boots and he could not dance very well so in the end we went to sit in the balcony.

He was straight from college and feeling rather ill for he had been vaccinated in one arm and innoculated in the other. His resistance, he always says, was very low at the time.

The next three evenings we sat on the grass along Sandylands catching up on our twenty years of life.

We were married in just under two years, on his embarkation leave but he did not go abroad until November 1942 when he, and some others, landed in North Africa and the war took a turn for the better.

We knew that Granny had accepted Norman as part of the family when she made a certain adjustment to her evening prayer.

"God bless the man, the woman and the child, and that there young lad in the Air Force, and bring him back safe."

God must have been attending for He did bring him back 'safe' though it took three long years.

Joyce marries, April 1942

Chapter 18 "Please, God, take me home."

Father would not buy anything on the black market and the only extra we had was an occasional boiling fowl from a local chicken farm where we had regularly bought poultry and eggs in the past.

Our town lunches helped with the rations and Mother's habit of squirrelling away material made it possible in those first years to have clothes made, off ration.

Before the war I had been totally disorganised and careless about silk stockings and if they had a small hole or ladder I would toss them into a drawer and buy another pair. These rejects were now very precious. I would wear odd ones, neatly darned, and ladders were painstakingly mended with a tiny gadget which picked up dropped stitches.

By comparison with many people our lives were easy and reasonably comfortable. Norman, as far as I knew, was safe, though many of the boys I had known had been killed or injured.

Dear Uncle Tom, who had taught me to drive, died of pneumonia just after his fiftieth birthday while he was waiting to be recalled to the Navy.

There was an awful weariness about life for it seemed as if the war would go on forever.

Granny had had her ninetieth birthday in the spring of 1943. She had always been thin but now her arms had a skeleton-like look. Her hair, cut short now but still thick, framed her fleshless face.

She would sit for long hours with her eyes closed seeming to cut off from life, immobile except for the constant movement of her foot.

Now in her nightly prayer she pleaded, "Please God, take me home."

As another winter came on Mother kept her in bed for longer each day, much to Granny's annoyance. She had never been one for lying in bed, not in my lifetime anyhow. "They dee i' bed," she was fond of saying.

For several days she had not been well but on this Saturday she had insisted on being dressed and was sitting by the fire when I reached home about half past one. It was December and nearing Christmas and very foggy.

That morning Father had 'cleared a mouth' with a doctor there to give the anaesthetic. They had been very difficult extractions and in the evening the man's wife rang to say he was still bleeding badly and would Father go to see him.

The man lived at the far side of town in the Wakefield Road area and as the fog was very bad I went with him. Fog was bad at any time but in the black out and with car lights only showing tiny slits it was well nigh impossible to see.

It was even worse in town and we drove twice round the Town Hall before we found Wakefield Road. We had difficulty locating the house but, after what seemed like hours, we arrived there.

Father plugged the bleeding sockets and then we had to wait to make sure that the blood had coagulated and finally stopped. Then we started the journey home.

The only way he could manage was for me to lean out of the open window directing him to keep his left wheels in the gutter. It was well after midnight when we finally arrived home and Mother was frantic with worry.

Earlier she had persuaded Granny to go to bed and it was obvious now that she was very ill. Next morning she was worse, while I started a severe attack of influenza.

In those first days I could barely lift my head from the pillow and I felt guilty that I could do little to help with Granny. She never lost consciousness but refused all food and drink.

The day I struggled downstairs again I heard her say to the doctor, "I'm bahn to dee this time. They don't want me here."

That hurt, for though they had had their differences Mother had cared for her long and faithfully. Yet I still could not believe that Granny would die.

For as long as I could remember Granny had had her grave clothes ready, a white cotton nightgown with insertions of crochetwork, which Mother washed and starched each year.

That last Friday evening Granny nipped out of bed to use her chamber pot as usual, and a short while afterwards she just closed her eyes and died.

Dear old Granny, she had cared for and nursed so many people in her long life, but she took no nursing, she just accomplished it all very neatly.

Dr Whitely had been a poor prophet. It had been a very long six months.

That night Mother helped the nurse lay out Granny in the special nightdress and then she took the dog for his walk. When she came back she had been crying.

"It suddenly came to me," she said. "I have no mother."

I was not well enough to go to Granny's funeral that cold day just before Christmas. They took her to Thornton and put her in the grave where her father, her mother and her sister, Hagah, already were.

Granny was the last one and Mother, seeing that the gravestone was leaning, suggested that they put it flat down on the grave. Later when we went to put flowers on her grave Mother was upset to discover they had put the stone with the inscription downwards so there is now no way of knowing where she lies.

I have no idea where all her clothing went, those heavy woollen dresses and cardigans, so different from the thick silk gowns she had once loved. Those drawers, two tube-like legs with frills, set on a buttoned waist band, which had so embarrassed me when they blew on the line, would be museum pieces now.

Gone were the knee length woollen vests, the grey corsets which bulked out her frail body, the woollen stockings which invariably wrinkled down into her flat shoes.

Yet I can see her still, sitting there, old and frail and somehow indestructible, moving her foot up and down, up and down.

They say the dead never die so long as someone remembers them. Indeed as I write this, Granny, and all those others, seem very close to me.

Chapter 19 The Family

My father died when he was eighty-seven just a few months before Vicky, our first grandchild, was born.

Just before he died he said to my husband, "Life is amazing, one going out and another new life coming in."

Mother lived for sixteen more years to love and nurse all her eight great-grandchildren. Her last years were difficult ones and like her mother before her she entreated God to 'take her home'.

Her funeral was on a brilliant day in June and I was determined that it would not be a sad affair but rather a celebration of a life. Seven of our grandchildren were there.

It was a month before her ninety-seventh birthday. I asked our son, David, to speak, and this is part of what he said.

"When Mum asked me to speak at Granny's funeral I found that I could not just talk about her life without including my grandfather's too. Most people here knew them as a couple and many memories of George and Lena will stay with us as long as we live.

"It has been said that things were not always easy between my grandparents and even as a child I sensed this tension. Granny could be so annoyingly 'nit picking' whilst Grandpa was rather cool, fastidious and dogmatic.

"Yet I also knew in my heart that it was more than habit that had kept them together through a life with its share of difficulties and sorrows. They had a real commitment and love for each other.

"Whilst I grew up Granny and Grandpa were always just down the road, perhaps sometimes too near, yet I understand now how little I valued the advantages of that closeness. Whenever I wanted I could 'pop' in to see them and would always be welcomed and would be given bovril and biscuits.

"Elizabeth, Marianne and I could explore from cellar to attic and Granny never minded us rummaging through treasures stored in mysterious boxes and trunks.

"I still have a thick leather labourer's belt with a fine brass buckle which belonged to an uncle of Granny's, and my sisters also came away with little gifts which took their fancy.

"What I remember and now value the most were the times when I could talk to Granny and Grandpa when they were on their own. Granny's endless and encyclopaedic excursions into her past life often left me confused as to which relative did what. Despite this problem she could paint a vivid picture of the very different life that families experienced when she was young.

"If Grandpa was in the mood he was a wonderful companion and I can still remember the times when I sat with him in the comfortable living room and he would talk to me 'man to man', as he shared his deepest thoughts and philosophies with me.

"Over the years Mum has filled in a few background details and I began to understand what a remarkable grandfather I had, a very private and undemonstrative man with a great love for me and his family."

Family — that most important unit of human life. Sometimes when we are all together, the sixteen of us, I remember again that lonely child living in a world of grownups, after Mollie. And I am eternally grateful.